Swami Dayananda is a [illegible] scholar and teacher of Vedanta who is held in high esteem by the academic and traditional pundit alike. Having extensively studied the Upanishads, logic and Sanskrit grammar under the guidance of various teachers, his deep scholarship lends great clarity to his teaching. In addition, his style and vivid communication skills establish a remarkable rapport with his audiences, whether it be gatherings of several thousands which regularly attend his talks in India or seminars at universities all over the world.

Swami Dayananda has conducted several intensive teacher-training courses in the methodology of Vedanta at his ashrams in Rishikesh, India, and Pennsylvania, USA. Many of those trained by him are now in turn actively teaching Vedanta. Swami Dayananda himself travels indefatigably to all parts of the world, teaching and lecturing, unfolding the universal message of Indian philosophy.

The Teaching of the Bhagavad Gita

Swami Dayananda

VISION BOOKS
(Incorporating Orient Paperbacks)
New Delhi • Mumbai • Hyderabad

Also by Swami Dayananda

~

Introduction to Vedanta
Understanding the Fundamental Problem

www.vision**books**india.com

First Published 1989
33rd Printing 2023

ISBN 10: 81-7094-395-7
ISBN 13: 978-81-7094-395-2

Published by
Vision Books Pvt. Ltd.
(Incorporating Orient Paperbacks & CARING imprints)
24 Feroze Gandhi Road, Lajpat Nagar 3
New Delhi-110024, India.
Phone: (+91-11) 2984 0821 / 22
e-mail: visionbooks@gmail.com

Printed at
Ashim Print Line
38/2, 35 & 36 Sahibabad Industrial Area, Ghaziabad
Uttar Pradesh 201010, India.

CONTENTS

Foreword

The teaching of the Bhagavad Gita opens with this assurance: there is no cause for grief. The Gita addresses itself to the human problem of conflict and grief. The context of the teaching is Arjuna's particular situation which nevertheless stems from the sense of inadequacy that every human being feels. That inability of a person to face a particular situation arises from his or her lack of understanding of the fact that every topical problem arises from the fundamental human problem of the inadequate self. Unless one discovers oneself to be an adequate self, life continues to be a problem. Lord Kṛṣṇa in the Bhagavad Gita reveals that every human being — in fact every being — is a complete, adequate self. The sense of inadequacy arises from the ignorance of the real nature of the self. A situation gets to be a problem and creates conflict and a feeling of helplessness. The knowledge of the self — and that knowledge alone — will eliminate the sense of inadequacy. When one discovers oneself to be a full and complete being, all the conflicts and grief vanish; happiness becomes natural, effortless; one becomes a spontaneous person; life becomes a sport. This knowledge is called *brahmavidyā* and is the principal teaching of the Bhagavad Gita. The Bhagavad Gita also teaches *karma yoga,* which is performance of action as an offering to the Lord and receiving its results as His grace. To appreciate the truth revealed by the scriptures, it is necessary to possess a contemplative mind, a mind that is free from likes and dislikes which are an obstacle to the knowledge of the self. Therefore, the Gita teaches *karma yoga* as a means of eliminating likes and dislikes. *Karma yoga* is nothing but *bhakti* or devotion to the Lord, which is expressed in the attitude of offering while performing an action and in the attitude of glad acceptance while receiving its result. This attitude of *yoga* neutralises likes and dislikes and brings about a mind that is tranquil and open – a learning mind. This is *yogaśāstra* and forms the secondary teaching of the Bhagavad Gita. *Brahmavidyā* and *yogaśāstra* together form the complete teaching of the Gita.

The effectiveness of the teaching of Lord Kṛṣṇa is evident from this declaration of Arjuna: "My confusion is gone. I have gained the knowledge that I am full and complete. I have no hesitation in doing what is to be done." This is what every one can say when the teaching of the Gita is assimilated.

In this book Swami Dayanandaji unfolds the teaching of the Gita in a lucid and direct language. While retaining the profundity of the text and the essence of the teaching in its entirety, Swamiji has made it simple and understandable to everyone. This being a condensed transcription of Sri Swamiji's talks on all the eighteen chapters of the Gita, the reader can have a total vision of the Gita as well as the individual, predominant topic discussed in each chapter.

The transcription was condensed and edited by Mrs. Candy Ramaswamy, California, a student of Sri Swamiji. We thank her for this great work. We also thank Susen Werner, Australia, also a student of Sri Swamiji, for her suggestions.

Swami Viditatmananda
For Sri Gangadhareswar Trust

1
The Human Problem

The human mind is a battlefield, a scene of constant conflict. The conflict arises only because choice is possible. An animal has no conflict; a cow does not wonder, "Should I be vegetarian or non-vegetarian?" Its life is governed by instinct. In this it has no choice. To choose is the privilege of a human being.

Conflicts arise when there is a choice: what to do, what to avoid, whether to be or not to be. One has to pause and think, again and again, because every moment one is at the crossroads and one cannot walk two roads. Should I do this or not? Should I act or renounce? Should I marry or not? An industrialist debates, "Should I build this plant or not?" A housewife asks, "Should I cook potatoes or eggplant?" Everyone has conflicts; every mind is a *kurukṣetra*, a battlefield.

The Fundamental Problem

It is a great blessing to be born a human being with the unique faculties of discrimination and choice. This blessing is also a curse, because choice creates conflicts. A person often turns to the Lord for help with those conflicts. A buffalo does not go to a temple or a church to pray or attend Mass. It neither seeks help, nor does it thank the Lord for the blessing received. Man, on the other hand, does all this with the hope of gaining inner strength. There appears to be no composure in a life that is full of problems which demand decisions. You just ask someone, "How are you?" and he will tell you his entire life story. This does not mean that he alone has problems; others know that this question is merely a formality and do not necessarily start telling their stories. Everyone has many woes to relate because every mind is a battlefield.

An animal is interested only in food and propagation; it

can instinctively take care of these needs. A human being also has the same needs, but he has an additional feature which creates problems for himself and others -- an unpredictable mind. In the morning he may feel good, but in the evening he may feel the opposite. One day he may be very friendly, but the next day he may be cantankerous and cannot accept even a small criticism, taking it as an insult. It is impossible for him to relate to others in a consistent way because he changes so frequently. Often he cannot relate properly even to himself. This problem of the changing mind, a mind in constant conflict, is not a problem of modern man alone; it is an ancient problem, a fundamental human problem.

The problem of the mind is not solved by satisfying all wants. Even if all wants could be fulfilled one would still have conflicts, wondering what to do next. Every day in deep sleep one calls for a truce to this inner battle but once the mind is awake, conflict starts again. Conflict remains as long as the mind remains, whether it is dreaming or awake.

One cannot live with conflict, nor can one solve conflict by temporarily desensitising the mind with drugs or other means; conflicts again loom large as soon as thinking commences. Am I to react to conflict by obliterating the power of the mind by losing my grip over it, by letting it revel in some state imagined to be free from the realities of life or should I attempt to find a solution to this conflict? In this matter a human being has no choice if he wants to retain control of his mind. The problem of conflict must be resolved for good.

The Desire To Be Different

The mind has extraordinary powers, and its suffering also is extraordinary. Beset by inner conflicts, when a man standing in the street sees a buffalo oblivious to the blowing horns he thinks, "Perhaps this buffalo is more blessed than I!" A buffalo is "happy" because it does not seem to be conscious of itself to be able to judge if it is happy or not. It lives according to its natural instincts without conflicts. It does not try to be different from what it is, since it does not have a self-consciousness in which it perceives itself as unhappy.

Wishing to be different is peculiar to human beings. Blessed with *buddhi,* the faculty of the intellect, a human being is not only conscious of the world, but also of himself. This is what distinguishes him from animals. It is the glory of man that he is conscious of himself. However the self he is aware of is not a complete, adequate self; it is, unfortunately, a wanting, inadequate self.

This wanting, inadequate self, the only self of which one is aware, is like *śruti*[1] in Indian music. The singer produces various melodies, but always keeps the voice in tune with *śruti,* the constant background drone of the *tamburā*[2] Similarly, behind all one's pursuits there is in one's heart a constant *śruti* which drones on, "I want...I want....I want...." This "I want" is a fundamental want, and it finds articulation in various specific wants, each an expression of the conclusion that one is an inadequate being.

This is the source of all conflict. In its desire to be complete, the mind, which is the platform for all undertakings, becomes a battlefield of conflicting ideas. There is always conflict, demanding solution. The human mind desires to be free from conflict.

Two Pursuits

When a person wants something, it is not an object that he or she really wants. Rather, by obtaining the object he hopes to be different. I am uneasy because I am not satisfied with myself as I am. Owing to the feeling that all is not well with me, I have to do something to set things right. A woman with a small pebble in her shoe, in whatever hurry she may be, has to stop and remove it in order to be comfortable. Similarly, there seems to be in the mind of each one of us an irritating bug that makes us strive to gain a sense of ease. To achieve this, one does exactly what others do, with small variations; one acquires certain desirable objects in order to be comfortable with oneself, or one gets rid of something undesirable, hoping that one will be happier in its absence.

---

1. The pitch in which any musical number is sung.

2. A musical instrument which holds the pitch in Indian music.

On reflection, all the pursuits undertaken in one's life fall under two categories, striving for something, and getting rid of certain other things. In Sanskrit, these are called *pravṛti* and *nivṛtti* respectively. In war the advance of the army is *pravṛiti* and withdrawal from the enemy in successful retreat is *nivṛtti*. Both types of pursuit are for the sake of one's comfort.

What one does to achieve comfort varies from individual to individual. One may want to get rid of a car which someone else is all too eager to buy. What one wants to acquire or get rid of is determined by one's values. What is common is that everyone wants to acquire or get rid of *something*. A person's desires keep on changing — a thing that was once desirable may no longer be so — yet what never changes is the *śruti*, "I want ...I want...I want...".

A wise man may just sit under a tree with the sky as his roof and the foliage of the tree as his ceiling. He does not want or need anything and is ready to give away what little he has, ready to give a passing dog the food that was given to him. And yet he seems very happy. Looking at him, another may think, "Let me give up everything and also be happy." He may walk out of society, leaving behind the securities of the family, home, and job. By such *nivṛtti* he does not necessarily become a happy man. Instead he may become a miserable beggar. Whereas previously he was mentally impoverished, now he has become materially impoverished as well. His position is worse than before.

There is another type of person who thinks, "If I have more, I will be happy. "More" is a comparative term. There can always be *more* of whatever one has..A man living on the street thinks he will be happy if he has two good meals a day. If he gets them, he will say, "Mere eating is not all that is to life." He wants to achieve something more to make him happy - a hut, then a flat, a house with a garden; a bicycle, a scooter, a car and finally a limousine. What next? He still remains the same inadequate self. He will have to roll up his sleeves and discover something else to become adequate. He may go places where he has not been before, but this will not satisfy him. Wherever he goes he will find only a rearrangement of what he has already seen — trees, rivers, birds , snow, people, sky, stars. Therefore, he will think, "I have already seen this. What else is there?" This *pravṛtti* is endless. Whatever one does, the droning "I want" remains.

This is the fundamental human problem. I long to feel at home, and to feel at peace with myself. Nowhere do I find that peace, because I am conscious of myself as an inadequate being and I cannot be at home with inadequacy. Not knowing how to solve the problem, I run away from it. At times, I listen to music in order to escape from sorrow. I may go to a movie to escape from the reality of my mind, hoping to gain solace. Nobody has ever solved a problem by escape. The problem of being conscious of a wanting self is not going to be solved by either *pravṛtti* or *nivṛtti*.

The Purpose of Life

Life is lived in the tension of want and inadequacy. You may think someone else is happy because he has comforts. This is because you have set a value for what he has. Nobody is really happy. The only difference between the "haves" and "have-nots" is that the "haves" are unhappy *with* comforts and the "have-nots" are unhappy *without* comforts. Everyone wants to be different from what he or she is. This is a problem common to every human being.

Solving this problem is the purpose of life. One cannot be indifferent to it. The experiences of life make one think, "What I want is not all these things. I want to be at ease with myself. How can I discover that?" When the problem is thus identified, one knows exactly what one should look for, and life becomes purposeful. Then alone it is worth living.

The Solution in the Gita

A relevant question is often asked, "What can the Gita do to solve my problems?" The Gita cannot give you food or shelter. It does not talk of the population explosion or of pollution control, because it is not meant for solving topical problems such as these. The Gita addresses itself to the problem of the inadequate self, because of which we are unable to face topical problems.

Topical problems come and go; the morning may bring you one problem, the evening another. Nobody, not even Vyāsa or Lord Kṛṣṇa, was free from topical problems. If such problems and challenges did not exist, life would become sheer monotony. A man complaining of problems is like the villager who complained of the miserliness of a wealthy soccer promoter who provided only one ball for twenty-two players. The ball must be one and the contenders many; then only is there a game. So, too, with the game of life. Only if there are challenges, will you enjoy it. For any individual or a nation there will be certain topical problems which are extremely difficult to solve, but the challenges can be met if one has a mind that is awake, that learns with every passing experience.

All topical problems can be handled better if we solve the fundamental problem. Otherwise while solving the current problems, we create new ones. How can a person who feels inadequate serve others? To serve others one must know oneself as an adequate person.

The problem of inadequacy is as old as humankind. It is the problem faced in the Gita by Arjuna, a warrior-hero of fabulous achievements and disciplined intellect, who was nevertheless overwhelmed by personal conflict and a feeling of helplessness. Lord Kṛṣṇa taught him how to know the adequate self. When he knew it, all his conflict and sorrow were resolved. This is the subject matter of the Bhagavad Gita.

The Gita is not meant for any one person or creed or nation; it is meant for humanity. It speaks to a mind that has fought in life, a mind that is dissatisfied with constant want, a mind that is alert and thinking and that has many conflicts. In the following chapters we will see that the Gita has the solution to the fundamental human problem of conflict and want. Like Arjuna, you too will say, "*Naṣṭo mohah!*" — gone is my delusion. This is the promise of the Gita.

2
The Sorrow of Arjuna

Behind all one's pursuits, the basic problem that remains unresolved is the feeling of inadequacy. Arjuna discovered this when he was faced with the prospect of a fratricidal war. He saw clearly that he would not find happiness either in victory or in defeat. His mind thus yearned for a solution to this fundamental human problem.

The Setting of the Gita

Lord Kṛṣṇa was a king who was hailed as God incarnate. However, his life was not easy. He was born in a prison and could not live with his own parents. Instead he was brought up by a cowherd chieftain. Even as a baby he had to face many enemies. Yet, for all his trials he was a happy person. Stories of his life narrated in the Mahābhārata, the Bhāgavata and other Purāṇas tell us about this.

Arjuna, a contemporary of Lord Kṛṣṇa, was one of the five Pāṇḍavas, the sons of Pāṇḍu. When these brothers inherited their father's vast kingdom, Dharmaputra, the eldest, became king. Arjuna and his brothers — Bhīma, Nakula and Sahadeva — were princes in name, disposition, and conduct. Unfortunately, these virtues did not extend to the entire family. Pāṇḍu's elder brother Dhṛtarāṣṭra had one hundred sons. The names of many of them began with the prefix *dur*, which means evil, and they lived true to their names. Duryodhana, the eldest of them, wanted for himself Dharmaputra's kingdom. He won it by cheating the Pāṇḍavas in a game of dice. According to the terms of the game, the defeated Dharmaputra and his brothers were to live in a forest for twelve years, and live incognito for another year. After thirteen years, they could return to claim their kingdom.

The Pāṇḍavas survived their exile and returned to their kingdom, but Duryodhana refused to honour his bargain. He would not relinquish the throne. Out of sympathy for Duryodhana and hoping to avoid a fratricidal war, the Pāṇḍavas sent Lord Kṛṣṇa to ask for at least a share of the kingdom. Duryodhana would not compromise. Lord Kṛṣṇa begged him for half the kingdom, or five villages, or a village with five houses, or at least a house with five rooms. All the proposals were rejected. Duryodhana said, "The Pāṇḍavas have lived for thirteen years in forest. Let them go back to the forest and spend the rest of their lives there. If they really want the land, they must win it by sword and, if they fight for it, they will get it only at my death."

Duryodhana was thus a usurper. As princes, the Pāṇḍavas not only had a right to the kingdom, but also had a duty to see that justice was done. They were willing to compromise to avoid a war, but this was not possible because of Duryodhana's greed. War was declared. A few great men who were dedicated to the cause of *dharma*, the moral and ethical code of the land, supported the Pāṇḍavas. Among them was Lord Kṛṣṇa, who served as Arjuna's charioteer.

Before the beginning of the battle, both Arjuna and Duryodhana had gone to Lord Kṛṣṇa seeking his help in the war. Lord Kṛṣṇa felt bound to oblige both. He told them, "I will neither take up any weapon nor fight for either side; on the other hand my army is fully equipped. You have a choice between my army and me." Duryodhana promptly wanted the army, and so when Arjuna chose to have Lord Kṛṣṇa on his side, he thought Arjuna foolish and congratulated himself on his good fortune.

Arjuna looked at things differently. He was confident that Lord Kṛṣṇa would make the difference between success and failure, because he considered Śrī Kṛṣṇa to be the Lord. Three factors determine the result of an action: *prayatna* - human endeavour; *kāla* - time; and *daivam* - the Lord. The first two factors are within one's control, but it is *daivam,* the unknown third factor, that makes the difference between success and failure. Arjuna had faith in *daivam;* Duryodhana did not. Because of the difference in their sense of values both were happy with what they received from Lord Kṛṣṇa.

Arjuna did not want to lose sight of Lord Kṛṣṇa; so he begged him to be the driver of his chariot, confident that with the Lord in the driver's seat, he would undoubtedly attain his objective.

The Opening Scene

As the armies assemble in the battlefield, in his palace the old, blind king Dhṛtarāṣṭra asks his minister, Sañjaya, what is happening:

धर्मक्षेत्रे कुरुक्षेत्रे समवेता युयुत्सवः ।
मामकाः पाण्डवाश्चैव किमकुर्वत सञ्जय ॥ १-१ ॥

Dharamakṣetre kurukṣetre samaveta yuyutsavaḥ
Māmakāh pāṇḍavāścaiva kimakurvata sañjaya (I:1)

O Sañjaya, assembled in the sacred field of Kurukṣetra, desiring to fight, what did my people and the Pāṇḍavas do?

By the two words *māmakāh* (my people) and pāṇḍavāḥ (the sons of Pāṇḍu), Dhṛtarāṣṭra's blindness is clearly revealed to be more than mere sightlessness. His distinguishing the Pāṇḍavas from "my people" reveals that he regards them as strangers, even though Pāṇḍu, their father, was his younger brother.

Dhṛtarāṣṭra's question seems silly. There already have been usurping, cheating at dice and banishing, which have culminated in the declaration of war. Warriors, armed to the teeth, have assembled in the battlefield to fight each other. What could one expect to happen on the battlefield? Certainly not an exchange of pleasantries. The underlying hope behind Dhṛtarāṣṭra's question is that, since the Pāṇḍavas are committed to *dharma* and since the country is a land where *dharma* is most sacred, perhaps they would decide to withdraw from the war and return to the forest. This would permit Duryodhana to retain the kingdom without an arrow being shot. The goodness of the Pāṇḍavas might benefit himself and his sons.

Sañjaya had been given the gift of telegnosis by Maharṣi Veda Vyāsa so that he could remain in the palace with the old king and narrate to him the happenings on the battlefield. Sañjaya's narration of the activity on the battlefield begins with the second verse:

दृष्ट्वा तु पाण्डवानीकं व्यूढं दुर्योधनस्तदा ।
आचार्यमुपसङ्गम्य राजा वचनमब्रवीत् ॥ १–२ ॥
अत्र शूरा महेष्वासा भीमार्जुनसमा युधि ।
युयुधानो विराटश्च द्रुपदश्च महारथः ॥ १–४ ॥

Dṛṣṭvā tu pāṇḍavānīkaṁ vyūḍhaṁ duryodhanastadā
Ācāryamupasaṅgamya rājā vacanamabravīt (I:2)

Atra śūrā maheṣ vāsā bhīmārjunasamā yudhi
Yuyudhāno virāṭaśca drupadaśca mahārathaḥ (I:4)

Seeing the army of the Pāṇḍavas, Duryodhana approached his teacher Droṇa, and said, "Here are the heroes, great archers, who are equal in battle to Arjuna and Bhīma: Yuyudhāna, Virāta, Drupada, all *mahārathas*.

A *mahāratha* is the commander of 11,000 archers. Arjuna was the object of all eyes among these great warriors in the Pāṇḍava ranks. Duryodhana here addresses Droṇa, who had taught archery to the Pāṇḍavas as well as the sons of Dhṛtarāṣṭra. Fearing that Droṇa might refuse to fight Arjuna, who was his best and most beloved disciple, Duryodhana praises Droṇa and the other great men who were assembled to fight on his side:

भवान्भीष्मश्च, कर्णश्च कृपश्च समितिञ्जयः ।
अश्वत्थामा विकर्णश्च सौमदत्तिस्तथैव च ॥ १–८ ॥

अन्ये च बहवः शूरा मदर्थे त्यक्तजीविताः ॥ १–९ ॥

Bhavānbhīṣmaśca karṇaśca kṛpaśca samitiñjayaḥ
Aśvatthāmā vikarnaśca saumadattistathaiva ca (I:8)

Anye ca bahavaśśūrā madarthe tyaktajīvitāḥ (I:9)

You, Bhīṣma, Karṇa, Kṛpa, who is victorious in war, Aśvatthāmā, Vikarṇa, the son of Somadatta, and many other valiant men who have forsaken their lives for my sake.

Duryodhana does not forget to mention Droṇa's son, Aśvatthāmā, because Droṇa has a weakness for his son which will later be the cause of his death. By calling these men *tyaktajīvitāḥ,* those who have forsaken their lives, Duryodhana, though unaware, revealed the outcome of the war.

He continues:

अपर्याप्तं तदस्माकं बलं भीष्माभिरक्षितम् ।
पर्याप्तं त्विदमेतेषां बलं भीमाभिरक्षितम् ॥ १-१० ॥

Aparyāptaṁ tadasmākaṁ balaṁ bhīṣmābhirakṣitaṁ
Paryāptaṁ tvidameteṣāṁ balaṁ bhīmābhirakṣitaṁ

(I:10)

Our army is insurmountable, protected by Bhīṣma, whereas the army commanded by Bhīsma is limited.

Duryodhana assures Droṇa, "With great men like yourself and Bhīṣma leading us, we have the advantage and we will surely prevail."

The war is about to begin. Bhīṣma, Droṇa, and the others in Duryodhana's army blow their conches. The music of martial instruments and the clang of weapons rend the air and shake the earth. Immediately the Pāṇḍava army responds:

पाञ्चजन्यं हृषीकेशो देवदत्तं धनञ्जयः ।
पौण्ड्रं दध्मौ महाशङ्खं भीमकर्मा वृकोदरः ॥ १-१५ ॥

Pāñcajanyaṁ hṛsīkeśo devadattaṁ dhanañjayaḥ
Pauṇḍraṁ dadhmau mahāśaṅkhaṁ bhīmakarmā vṛkodaraḥ

(I:15)

Lord Kṛṣṇa blew his conch, the Pāñcajanya; Arjuna blew his conch Devadatta, and Bhīma, who was called Vṛkodrara — one whose belly is like that of a wolf — blew his conch, Pauṇḍra

Arjuna's Conflict

The enemy forces are arrayed in battle; among them are the great warriors who had befriended Duryodhana. In order to see them better, Arjuna asks Kṛṣṇa:

सेनयोरुभयोर्मध्ये रथं स्थापय मेऽच्युत ॥ १-२१ ॥

Senayorubhayormadhye ratham̐ sthāpaya me'cyuta (I:21)

O Acyuṭa, please place my chariot between the two armies.

Lord Kṛṣṇa then takes Arjuna's chariot to a place from which Arjuna can see Droṇa, Bhīṣma, Karṇa, and the rest of his opponents. It is then that full realisation of who he has chosen to fight against dawns upon Arjuna. The magnitude of the event hits him. He thinks "Here is Bhīṣma, my grandfather, on whose lap I learned the alphabet; here is Droṇa, from whom I learned archery; here is Acārya Kṛpa. How can I fight with these people?" His resolve to fight melts. Seeing that those on the side of Duryodhana are his own people, Arjuna says to Lords Kṛṣṇa, "How can I fight my own family? I could never be happy killing those on whose company my happiness depends. I know such men won't ever consider retreat; they will fight to win or die in the battle. I cannot gain victory without destroying them, nor can I accept defeat. My heart is heavy now and will become heavier if I kill them. What then is to be gained by this war? I will let them have the kingdom even though it is rightfully ours."

Arjuna continues, "One may argue that it is not a question of gaining a kingdom, but of protecting *dharma*. I don't think that would be accomplished either, for *dharma* has to abide in people, and if I kill all these good men, there will be nobody to preserve or teach *dharma*. I see in this war only sin and the destruction of the society." He says:

न काङ्क्षे विजयं कृष्ण न च राज्यं सुखानि च ।
किं नो राज्येन गोविन्द किं भोगैर्जीवितेन वा ॥ १-३२ ॥
येषामर्थे काङ्क्षितं नो राज्यं भोगाः सुखानि च ।
त इमेऽवस्थिता युद्धे प्राणांस्त्यक्त्वा धनानि च ॥ १-३३ ॥

निहत्य धार्तराष्ट्रान्नः का प्रीतिः स्याज्जनार्दन ॥ १-३६ ॥

Na kāṅkṣe vijayam̐ kṛṣṇa na ca rājyam̐ sukhāni ca
Kim̐ no rājyena govinda kim̐ bhogairjīvitena vā (I:32)

Yeṣāmarthe kāṅksitam̐ no rājyam̐ bhogāṣsukhāni ca
Ta ime'vasthitā yuddhe prāṇām̐styaktvā dhanāni ca (I:33)

Nihatya dhārtarāṣtrannaḥ kā prītissyājjanārdana (I:36)

I don't want victory O Kṛṣṇa, nor kingdom nor comforts. Of what use is a kingdom or pleasures or even life? Those for whose sake I would desire all these things, are arrayed here in battle, ready to give up their lives and wealth.... Having killed the sons of Dhṛtarāṣṭra, what happiness will there be for me, O Janārdana?

Arjuna feels that any pleasures which may be gained through the impending war would be tainted by the death of Bhīṣma and others whom he loves. He had not bargained for this when he had vowed to fight. The chapter ends with Sañjaya's description of Arjuna's collapse:

एवमुक्त्वार्जुनः सङ्ख्ये रथोपस्थ उपाविशत् ।
विसृज्य सशरं चापं शोकसंविग्नमानसः ॥ १–४७ ॥

Evamuktvārjunassaṅkhye rathopastha upāviśat
Visṛjiya saśaraṁ cāpaṁ śokasaṁvignamānasaḥ (I:47)

Having spoken thus, casting aside his bow and arrows in the midst of the battle, Arjuna sat down in the chariot, his mind filled with grief.

Arjuna is confused and overwhelmed by sorrow. He sees no solution to his problem. He cannot decide whether to retreat *(nivṛtti)*, or advance *(pravṛtti)*. The proper course of action eludes him because of his own inadequacy: but he has faith that Lord Kṛṣṇa will help him find an answer. That answer is contained in the next seventeen chapters of the Gita.

3

The Search for Solution

The first chapter of the Gita — called *Arjuna-viṣāda-yoga,* the Sorrow of Arjuna — presents Arjuna as a person who cannot see what the right action is in the situation he faces. Even though he is a warrior who never shirked battle, he finds it impossible to fight when he sees his own people on either side. Arjuna is convinced that the war will bring destruction to both sides and make victory meaningless. He knows deep within himself that it is his duty to see that an evil-doer is punished, but the evil-doer in this case is Duryodhana, his own cousin; and aligned with him are many of Arjuna's relatives and friends. Thus there is a conflict between duty and personal bonds; there is confusion between reason and emotion.

Lord Kṛṣṇa's Advice

The second chapter of the Gita — called *Sāṅkhya-yoga,* the chapter on Knowledge — begins with Sañjaya, the commentator of the events in the battlefield, saying:

तं तथा कृपयाविष्टमश्रुपूर्णाकुलेक्षणम् ॥
विषीदन्तमिदं वाक्यमुवाच मधुसूदनः ॥ २-१ ॥

कुतस्त्वा कश्मलमिदं विषमे समुपस्थितम् ।
अनार्यजुष्टमस्वर्ग्यमकीर्तिकरमर्जुन ॥ २-२ ॥

क्लैब्यं मा स्म गमः पार्थ नैतत्त्वय्युपपद्यते ।
क्षुद्रं हृदयदौर्बल्यं त्यक्त्वोत्तिष्ठ परन्तप · ॥ २-३ ॥

Taṁ tathā kṛpayāviṣṭamaśrupūrṇākulekṣaṇaṁ
Viṣīdantamidaṁ vākyamuvāca madhusūdanaḥ (II:1)

Kutastvā kaśmalamidaṁ viṣame samupasthitaṁ
Anāryajuṣṭamasvargyamakīrtikarmarjuna (II:2)

Klaibyaṁ mā sma gamaḥ pārtha naitattvavyyupapadyate
Kṣudraṁ hṛdayadaurbalyaṁ tyaktvottiṣṭha parantapa

(II:3)

To the despondent (Arjuna) who was thus overwhelmed by sympathy and whose eyes were agitated and full of tears, Lord Kṛṣṇa said: "How has this depression come upon you at this inopportune time? This behaviour is not worthy of a noble man. It will not take you to heaven; it will only bring you ill-fame. Do not give in to unmanliness, O Pārtha;[1] It is not proper for you. Giving up this lowly weakness of heart, get up, O Parantapa."[2]

In these verses Lord Kṛṣṇa is only advising Arjuna. He has not yet begun to teach him. He uses words designed to shake Arjuna and spur him to action. Arjuna's decision not to fight could be interpreted as one born of fear. Lord Kṛṣṇa wants to make him think. "You are placed in a situation where you are supposed to act, not talk, and you have pulled me in, too. What you are now saying does not reflect your culture and upbringing. Your action is not becoming of an *ārya*, a noble man who does what is to be done. Withdrawal from the battlefield will give you neither fame nor heaven. How did you arrive at the conclusion that it would be sinful to fight this battle? What constitutes sin is known through Dharmaśastra[3] which reveals that a soldier who runs away from the battlefield commits a sin. He will not better his lot here on earth, much less will he go to heaven.

"If you argue that you do not care for what happens after death, that you are a practical man who only wants to live a few years, getting as much as he can out of this earthly life, even then this kind of action will not help you. All the fame for which you have worked so assiduously will come to naught because of this single action. Everyone will talk of you as the great warrior who ran away from the battlefield; you will be laughed at as a great archer with a coward's heart. They will forget that you were a mighty man and will only

---

1, 2. Epithets of Arjuna. Pārtha literally means "one born of the earth", and Parantapa, "the destroyer of enemies".
3. The scriptural texts describing the nature of *dharma*.

talk about you in words that would sully my tongue were I to utter them."

अवाच्यवादांश्च बहून्वदिष्यन्ति तवाहिताः ।
निन्दन्तस्तव सामर्थ्यं ततो दुःखतरं नु किम् ॥ २-३६ ॥

Avācyavādaṁsca bahūn vadiṣyanti tavāhitāḥ
Nindantastava sāmarthyaṁ tato duhkhataraṁ nu kim

(II:36)

Your enemies will say many unspeakable things, scorning your prowess; what could cause greater sorrow than this?

Lord Kṛṣṇa continues to paint a bleak picture for Arjuna. "You may think of retiring to a remote corner of the Himālayas, leaving it to the Lord or chance to provide you with food; but people who will come there for pilgrimage, recognising you sitting under a tree, will remember you as a useless fellow, a chicken-hearted, spineless creature. If you were an ordinary soldier, no one, except your wife, would know that you had fled from battle; but if you run away, it is not going to be that simple. Your entire army will follow you and Duryodhana will win the battle without firing a shot. A despot like Duryodhana will see to it that this message is proclaimed to everyone: 'Seeing the formation of my army, Arjuna ran away from the battlefield, not out of compassion, but out of fear.'

"Therefore, do not let this unmanliness overwhelm you, Arjuna; it does not behove you. It may be acceptable to someone else, but to you, a Pāṇḍava prince, it is not. If you run away from your duty, who else will perform it? Stand by your post and do what is expected of you. Give up this weakness of heart. Arise, live up to your title, Parantapa, the destoryer of enemies. Do not abuse your name or the name of *dharma.*"

Arjuna's Discovery of the Problem

Lord Kṛṣṇa's words stir Arjuna's heart. Arjuna, who does not even know the spelling of the word fear, who has never been afraid of anything in his life, and who has always defended and asserted his self-respect within the framework of *dharma* is being called *klība,* a eunuch. Stung, Arjuna says:

"I do not deserve these words, O Lord! You know that very well. I am not a coward. I am a brave man and a brave man can have sympathy and attachment and compassion." Arjuna tries to explain his case to Lord Kṛṣṇa:

कथं भीष्ममहं सङ्ख्ये द्रोणं च मधुसूदन ।
इषुभिः प्रतियोत्स्यामि पूजार्हावरिसूदन ॥ २-४ ॥

Katham bhīṣmamaham saṅkhye droṇam ca madhusūdana
Iṣubhiḥ pratiyotsyami pūjarhāvarisudana (II:4)

O Madhusūdana,[1] how can I fight with arrows in battle against Bhīṣma and Droṇa who deserve to be worshipped, O Arisūdana?[2]

The cause of Arjuns'a torment is clear: "These people are not mere acquaintances or relatives; they are *pūjārha,* those who deserve to be worshipped. They are the people on whose laps I sat and from whom I gained all my skills and knowledge. How can I fight them? I cannot shoot pointed arrows at them. They deserve flowers. You may ask, 'If they don't have any qualms about fighting you in this war, why should you have such tender feelings?' I can only say, let them cast their lot with Duryodhana and fight against me. I would rather be killed by them than raise a hand against them."

Sometimes one can help solve another person's problems by simply listening patiently. While the person is talking, he or she has to think, and in the process, the muddled thoughts may be straightened out. Lord Kṛṣṇa is listening attentively, as Arjuna's pattern of thinking changes:

गुरूनहत्वा हि महानुभावान्
श्रेयो भोक्तुं भैक्ष्यमपीह लोके ॥ २-५ ॥

Gurūnahatvā hi mahānubhāvān
śreyo bhoktum bhaikṣyamapīha loke (II:5)

1&2. Titles of Lord Kṛṣṇa. Madhusūdana literally means destroyer of the demon Madhu which stands for the ego; Arisūdana means destroyer of enemies.

Better to live on alms in this world than kill these teachers who are worthy of great respect.

Until now Arjuna has been thinking only of the horror of killing Bhīṣma, Droṇa, and the others. Now he begins to think of alternatives. His thoughts turn to the life of *bhikṣus, mendicants,* who retire to the forest, live a simple life in pursuit of truth and depend on alms for sustaining their life.

A person who commits himself to the pursuit of knowledge is generally supported by the society which values knowledge. In the modern society scientists are provided with grants and resources for research, being told, in effect, "You may or may not discover anything; your hypothesis may prove wrong; it does not matter. Continue your research — that is enough." Society will not disown a person who pursues knowledge. In this way Indian society supports *bhikṣus,* mendicants, who dedicate their life to the pursuit of the knowledge of the Self.

With the thought, "I would rather live on *bhikṣā* than fight," a new line of thinking is triggered in Arjuna's mind. We all experience such reversals in our patterns of thought. For instance, an overwhelming event, like the death of a friend, may start a chain of inquiry, "This man was alive yesterday. He is dead now. What happened to his life? Was he just the body, or was there something different from the body which left the body and for which the body died? Is there something more profound, more lasting, than this physical body of flesh and bones? This man died, leaving everything behind. Am I also the same? Are all my wants and achievements meaningless? Should life be spent struggling if the outcome is death? Can't I resolve my struggles during my lifetime?" These questions are fundamental and universal and arise out of ignorance about ourselves.

Under the tense conditions of the battlefield Arjuna begins to appreciate this human problem. Confronted with the prospect of killing or being killed by his dearest relatives, he begins to think about the profundity of life and pettiness of regarding people and things as "my" and "mine" He tells Lord Kṛṣṇa,

न हि प्रपश्यामि ममापनुद्याद्
यच्छोकमुच्छोषणमिन्द्रियाणाम् ।
अवाप्य भूमावसपत्नमृद्धं
राज्यं सुराणामपि चाधिपत्यम् ॥ २–८ ॥

Na hi prapaśyāmi mamāpanudyād
yacchokamucchoṣaṇamindriyāṇāṁ
Avāpya bhūmāvaspatnamṛddhaṁ
rājyaṁ surāṇāmapi cādhipatyaṁ (II:8)

Indeed I cannot see what will remove the sorrow that dries up my senses, even if I gain on this earth an unrivalled and prosperous kingdom or even lordship over the gods.

Arjuna recognises the futility of trying to solve the fundamental problem of a wanting self by gaining wealth or power. "Even when kingdoms are won, there will be more kingdoms to exploit. How can one ever say 'I have achieved everything I want'? I don't see how any of these achievements can negate the sorrow, expressed or unexpressed, that is the constant companion of the human heart. The *śruti* of 'I want' will always go on."

Arjuna's mind seems to be clear now. He asks Lord Kṛṣṇa for help:

कार्पण्यदोषोपहतस्वभावः
पृच्छामि त्वां धर्मसम्मूढचेताः ।
यच्छ्रेयः स्यान्निश्चितं ब्रूहि तन्मे
शिष्यस्तेऽहं शाधि मां त्वां प्रपन्नम् ॥ २–७ ॥

Kārpaṇyadoṣopahatasvabhāvaḥ
pṛcchāmi tvāṁ dharmasammūḍhacetāḥ
Yacchreyassyānniścitaṁ brūhi tanme
śiṣyaste'haṁ śādhi māṁ tvāṁ prapannaṁ (II:7)

I, one whose nature has been tainted by miserliness, whose mind is confused about *dharma*, ask you. Please tell me definitely what is absolutely good. I am your disciple; please teach me; I seek refuge in you.

A *kṛpaṇa,* miser, is defined in the Bṛhadāraṇyak-opaniṣad

as one who leaves this world without knowing the truth about himself, for he has not used the vast wealth of human intellect to inquire into the purpose of human life. Arjuna, who has heard this word used in this way, says, "I have never made any real use of my intellect; when I am not even able to distinguish between *dharma* and *adharma,* what to talk of the knowledge of what is most fundamental in life? I have not understood all this because I have been miserly in using my intellect. But now I am not going to miss any opportunity to learn. Please be my *guru,* O Lord! I am your disciple, surrendering at your feet. Please bless me by teaching me that which is *śreyas."* Lord Kṛṣṇa had been a friend, philosopher, and guide to Arjuna throughout his life. Now he decided to be his teacher, at Arjuna's request.

What is this *śreyas* that Arjuna seeks to know? It is the common end sought by everyone - a freedom from any feeling of discomfort; the discovery of a pleased and complete being. *Śreyas* is not simply "what is good for oneself", as it is generally translated; it is the ultimate good that everyone seeks, knowingly or unknowingly.

Good is a relative word. What is good today may not be good tomorrow. There is no such thing as *the* good medicine — what is good depends upon the disease to be cured. Similarly, there is no action that is absolutely good. Taking into account a number of factors, one decides what action is right, i.e., *dharma*, and what action is wrong, i.e., *adharma,* in a partifular situation. In Indian culture there are no absolute dos or don'ts. Dharma is not absolute; sometimes *satyam,* speaking truth, or *ahimsā,* non-injury, must be sacrificed in a particular situation, to achieve overall good. This relativity of *dharma* is illustrated in the Purāṇas, collections of stories depicting the nature of *dharma.* As there is no absolute right or absolute wrong in this relative world, a sense of *dharma* has to grow within one. A person who understands *dharma* can decide upon an action appropriate to any situation, just as a good driver knows how to negotiate any new traffic situation.

While *dharma* is relative, *śreyas* is absolute; it is applicable to everyone. The objects and situations we seek are different, but what we hope to gain from our achievements is common to everyone; we want happiness, fullness, liberation, *pūrṇa ātmā* (the full self), *nirvāṇa* — all expressions meaning 'the pleased being', *śreyas*. One who gains this is happy with oneself, and happily goes about doing whatever must be done.

The impending war has taught Arjuna that in the relative world any gain must also involve a loss: by fighting he would gain kingdom but lose his family; by fleeing the battlefield he would save his loved ones, but sacrifice his fame and chance to enter heaven; and *dharma*, bereft of a champion, would fall. Seeing the limitations in both the alternatives, Arjuna realises that he wants only *śreyas*, the absolute gain that cannot be achieved by mere effort, no matter how heroic or righteous. He realises that he needs a *guru*, a teacher who is able to explain to him what *śreyas* is and how it is to be gained; and he requests Lord Kṛṣṇa to be his *guru*.

The Sanskrit word *guru* is defined as follows:

गुकारस्त्वन्धकारो वै रुकारस्तन्निवर्तकः ।
अन्धकारनिरोधित्वाद्गुरुरित्यभिधीयते ॥

Gukārastvandhakāro vai rukārastannivartakaḥ
Andhakāranirodhitvādgururityabhidhīyate

The syllable *gu* stands for darkness, and *ru* for the remover of that. Since he dispels darkness, (the teacher) is called *guru*.

The darkness here stands for ignorance. The one who dispels the darkness of ignorance by the light of knowledge is called *guru*.

Suppose an object in a room cannot be seen because the room is dark. If I bring a light into the room, I see the object. The light enables me to see something which was there all along. I have gained what was already there by the removal of my ignorance of it. This is how *śreyas* is to be gained. It is the knowledge of *śreyas* that Arjuna seeks from Lord Kṛṣṇa.

Arjuna finds his *guru* in Lord Kṛṣṇa; he surrenders to him, asking for knowledge of *śreyas*. Lord Kṛṣṇa accepts him as his disciple, and what he teaches helps Arjuna to solve his problem by solving the fundamental problem of humankind.

4
The Three Limitations

Everyone seeks freedom from his sense of inadequacy. This freedom is called *śreyas*. Arjuna wanted *śreyas* and to gain it he became Lord Kṛṣṇa's disciple.

No Cause for Sorrow

Lord Kṛṣṇa begins his teaching with a very reassuring statement:

अशोच्यानन्वशोचस्त्वं प्रज्ञावादांश्च भाषसे ।
गतासूनगतासूंश्च नानुशोचन्ति पण्डिताः ॥ २–११ ॥

Aśocyānanvaśocastvaṁ prajñāvādāṁśca bhāṣase
Gatāsūnagatāsūṁśca nānuśocanti paṇḍitāḥ (II:11)

You are grieving over that which deserves no grief, although you talk words of wisdom. The wise grieve neither for the living nor for the dead.

This is the eleventh verse of the second chapter. The earlier verses describe Arjuna's conflict, his analysis of the human problem and the consequent disinterest in wealth and power, and his turning to Lord Kṛṣṇa for a solution. This verse is the first verse of the Lord's teaching, and thus it is also considered the first verse of the Gita. Śrī Śaṅkarācārya begins his commentary on the Gita with this verse.

Lord Kṛṣṇa states plainly that there is no cause for sorrow. Although one is at times sorrowful, the Lord looks upon sorrow as an intruder, like a germ that has entered one's system. One cannot suffer a dust particle in the eye or a germ in the stomach. The system does not tolerate anything alien. It must be expelled. Sorrow, too, is intolerable to one, and this indicates that sorrow contradicts one's true nature. This may seem to be a bold statement; but is it not true that one does not want sorrow, that one seeks only happiness and freedom from sorrow? Just as a sick person wants first to get rid of his disease and then pursue pleasure, man longs for the absence of sorrow, and then for the presence of happiness, since sorrow is foreign to his nature.

The Limitations of a Human Being

Everyone suffers from a sense of limitation but no one accepts that, because one cannot be happy as a limited being. Through analysis we can identify three types of limitations. The first is the limitation of sorrow. Sometimes our sorrow is very eloquent, sometimes it is only an unwept sorrow; but the basis of sorrow, the feeling, "All is not well with me" is always there. That the human heart is subject to sorrow is a limitation no one wants to accept.

Another limitation that we feel is that of time. Nobody wants to die today; everyone wants to live a day longer. Animals and plants also have this love for life. Even a tree bends to grow towards the sun. Only if we find that this world can no longer give us happiness do we think of quitting it; if a person is healthy and happy, he or she wants to live on. Perhaps it is this love for continuity that accounts for the desire to have a son or a daughter, or urges one to engrave one's name on a stone. No one wants to disappear without leaving a trace.

We know that we shall all die one day, and yet we want to live for at least today. The desire to live today is the desire to be eternal; we do not want to admit that we are mortal, even though we know very well that our birth and death are marked on the sands of time. Mortality, a limitation with respect to time, is the second limitation that we cannot stand.

The third limitation that humankind suffers is ignorance. If a person is not enrolled in a school or a training institute, he or she will at least stand at the window to see what is happening in the street. This behaviour is an expression of our innate love for knowledge. We cannot stand ignorance; we always want to know something more.

If you examine all your pursuits, *pravṛtti* or *nivṛtti,* you will discover that all your life you have been trying to overcome these three limitations. You seem to have concluded that you are sorrowful, mortal, ignorant. You seek more security and more objects so that you can be comfortable in your life; much of your time is spent in going after things that are meant to make you happy, to keep sorrow at bay. Another part of your life is spent in pursuing things that will keep you going just one day more; you do exercises or take vitamins and proteins out of a desire to live a little longer. A third part of your life is spent gathering knowledge. For some, such as scientists, who regard knowledge as the most important goal in life, this is the most predominant pursuit, but everyone does devote a part of his or her life to learning. Picking up a newspaper in the morning is prompted by this quest for knowledge; reading the Gita is motivated by a desire to seek freedom from one's sense of inadequacy. Thus the three things we seek in all our pursuits are freedom from sorrow, freedom from death, and freedom from ignorance.

Illegitimate Problems

The Lord says that all the three limitations are illegitimate; that is, all three are *aśocya,* matters that do not warrant any grief. A problem can be solved only if it is legitimate. If you see a snake on the road you can choose to avoid it or chase it away, so that you can continue on the road. Encountering a snake is a legitimate problem and it can be solved by such actions. But if the problem looming large in your mind is illegitimate, how can you solve it by an act? Let us consider the famous example of a rope mistaken for a snake by an imaginative mind. The illegitimate, projected snake and the fear one experiences on seeing it cannot be removed by beating the snake or by throwing a stone or by praying or clapping. The snake and the fright caused by it will go away only when one comes to know that there is no snake in fact. When one sees the rope, the problem is solved and one's fear goes. In this case, one solves the problem not by action, but by knowledge. A legitimate problem can be solved by action but an illegitimate one can only be solved by knowing that it is illegitimate.

If I can make you see that a given problem does not really exist, I have released you from it. The knowledge that the limitations of sorrow, time, and ignorance do not really exist for you frees you from these limitations. That knowledge is called *sāṅkhya,* that which is clearly seen. It is unfolded by Vedanta. This knowledge is the subject matter of the second chapter of the Gita, and the subsequent chapters discuss either the same or allied topics.

Illegitimate Search

Lord Kṛṣṇa's statement that Arjuna's problem is illegitimate opens up a new line of inquiry. If his situation does not call for grief, why is Arjuna grieving? Arjuna feels touched by the sorrow of the situation, and so he is grieving; but can sorrow really touch us? We console a bereaved person because we think that one should not remain in sorrow. We do not want sorrow ever to visit us, or others, because we recognise sorrow as foreign to our nature. On the other hand, we do not console someone who is happy; instead we celebrate his or her happiness. We recognise happiness as something natural to us.

If sorrow is not really a part of you, and happiness alone is natural to you, why do you search for happiness outside yourself? You search because you do not know what you are. Like a person who searches for a lost key, only to find it in his or her pocket, you miss the happiness that is your own nature and search for it everywhere.

A man from a small Indian village once went to the market town to buy five donkeys. Since his village was quite far, he decided to ride back on the sturdiest of the donkeys, letting the others trail along. When he neared his home he wanted to make sure that all the five donkeys were still with him. He looked back and counted, and discovered that there were only four donkeys. He cursed himself for not paying closer attention to them during the journey, and arrived home in a dejected mood. As he was getting off the donkey he told his wife, who had come out to greet him, "I feel very sad. I bought five donkeys, but somehow I lost one on the way." The wife looked at him and remarked, "You are right. There aren't five donkeys, — there are six!" Similarly, a thing may be with you, but if you do not recognise it, you effectively disown it and go about searching for it. Such a search is an illegitimate one, to be solved only by knowing that the thing is, in fact, with you all the time.

Thus, Kṛṣṇa tells Arjuna that what he seeks does not

exist."You want to achieve freedom from the limitations of sorrow, mortality and ignorance because you do not know that this freedom is already achieved, just as the removal of the imagined rope-snake is already achieved. You need not do anything to remove the snake because it was never there. What exists, in fact, is only the rope, which cannot frighten you.

The Relative I

This is the nature of the human problem. The confusion is universal, because ignorance is universal. Everyone is born totally ignorant: when you were born you did not know even your father or mother. When your sense organs started operating, you began picking up knowledge and shedding ignorance, and this process continues throughout your life, aided by many teachers — father, mother, grandmother, preceptors. But in all your learning, what have you done to remove your ignorance about yourself?

A simple question will help you appreciate that you do not know who you really are. In everyday life any experience you have, brings out of you a certain person. Who is that person? Asked to describe your day, you might say, "In the morning I got up, I bathed, I ate breakfast, I went to the office, I ate lunch, I left the office, I came home, and I slept." One "I" did all these various activities. Do you really know anything about that "I"?

Every experience involves you, the experiencer. As you undergo various experiences, though you are the same in all of them, you present yourself differently to different people. For example, to your father you present yourself as a son, to your son as a father, to your wife as a husband, to your friend as a friend, to your employer as an employee. As you relate to each different person, you assume an appropriate, relative persona.

This is true not only in relation to people we encounter, but also in relation to objects, situations, and events. You do not relate in the same way to all objects; and towards the same object you act differently at different times. One day you watch the sun rising and you are happy; but the next day the same sunrise does not thrill you — you feel like going back to sleep although the sun is up and you have to rise and take care of your daily woes. There is nothing in life about which you can say, "I shall always like this." The one who likes is thus a relative I; the one who dislikes is also a relative I. So too, the frustrated I, the happy I, the bored I — all are only relative I's. Then, who are you fundamentally? Who are you, without reference to any of these mental states of happiness, frustration, anger, despair, boredom?

When you were young there was an I which said, "I am a child of ten." Then you became a teenager, then an adult, then middleaged, and now you are old. In all these physical states, the I is the same. The body keeps on changing but you are not the child, nor the adult. You are not the physical body which is subject to change. Lord Kṛṣṇa says:

देहिनोऽस्मिन्यथा देहे कौमारं यौवनं जरा ।
तथा देहान्तरप्राप्तिर्धीरस्तत्र न मुह्यति ॥ २–१३ ॥

Dehino'smin yathā dehe kaumāraṁ yauvanaṁ jarā
Tathā dehāntaraprāptirdhīrastatra na muhayati (II:13)

Just as the (self) embodied in this body must pass through childhood, youth, and old age, so too will it assume another body (at death); with reference to that the wise do not come to grief.

Lord Kṛṣṇa is saying, "This physical body is occupied in childhood, youth, and old age by only one I. In what you know as yourself — boy, youth, uncle, cousin — that I is common, assuming all these various roles in life, like an actor on the stage. An actor can appear in a variety of costumes, but from his face you can recognize him Similarly, in this physical body, there is one I that takes on the roles of boy, young man, and adult — an I that is the central being that informs all experiences, that plays different roles. Who is that central being?"

Suppose that in a play one actor plays the role of a king, and another the role of a beggar. Now while playing their roles, suppose that the first actor thinks that he really is a king and ignoring his script, occupies the throne on the stage and refuses to make an exit. The second actor thinks that he is really a beggar and goes about begging on or off the stage, forgetting the play entirely. Neither of these can play his role if he assumes that he really is that role. There is nothing wrong in playing a role as long as one *knows* that one is playing a role; it is not important whether one plays the role of a beggar or a king—both roles will be paid equally well. A problem occurs only if one forgets that one is playing a role and takes the role to be real. If an actor takes his role to be himself, the play becomes a mess.

This is the source of the fundamental problem. You assume a number of roles and forget the central being that there is in every role you play. Who is that being? Who am I, free from all the roles? If I cannot answer this question, I have a serious problem: I do not know the central being who informs all the roles that are being played. To answer the question "Who am I?" I must know that central being, the fundamental I.

The Fundamental I

I see the sky; it is an object of my perception. I see the stars; they are objects of my perception. I see you; you are an object of my perception. I perceive not only forms, but also sounds, smells, tastes, touches — all these are objects of my perception. Is the self, that central being that perceives all these, another object of perception, or is it the subject? It is the subject, and anything else becomes an object of its perception.

I am the subject who knows the world; everything I know is object. The knower of an object is different from the object. Therefore I am not an object; I am not any of the things I know. I may think of objects as "mine" but I never think of them as "I"; I may say, "This is my book, my watch, my child," but take none of these as myself. The truth of the fundamental I, the central being who sees the entire world, Lord Kṛṣṇa teaches Arjuna in the Gita. The freedom one gains by knowing this I is called *śreyas*.

5
Who Am I?

No form of ignorance is dispelled by itself; to remove ignorance one must gain knowledge, by making use of the valid means of knowledge. If I am ignorant of myself and want to know who I am, I must find some means of knowledge capable of making me know myself.

Words can reveal objects known and unknown and so they can be a valid means of knowledge,. Knowledge obtained by words can be direct or indirect. About an object that is away from you descriptive words can convey indirect knowledge, which has to be verified later — when the object becomes available to you — by another means of knowledge, such as perception.

When an object is with you but you do not recognise it, words can bring about direct knowledge of it. When you meet a friend whom you have not seen for ten years, you may not recognise him; but when he is introduced to you, the recognition is direct and immediate. Lord Kṛṣṇa uses words to give direct knowledge of the being which is central, but is not recognised because it plays so many roles in life.

Why You Are Ignorant of Yourself

You have no chance of knowing yourself in any of the three states of experience. In deep sleep you have definitely no chance of knowing yourself or anything else in the world. And while awake or in a dream, you continually shift from role to role, so that in school, at home or in the place of work you come to know yourself only as the relative I. Thus, there being no opportunity to know the fundamental I, you continue to remain ignorant of yourself. This ignorance is universal.

To gain knowledge of the self we must be taught as Arjuna was. With the help of this teaching, we start an inquiry into the question, "Who is this I?"

Everything you know is an object and you are the subject. There are only two things in creation: ***kṣetra,*** the object, and ***kṣetrajña*** the subject, the one who knows the object. This concept is discussed in detail in the thirteenth chapter of the Gita, but it is also unfolded in the second chapter.

Are You the Body?

We know that objects are not I, because we do not have any I-sense in them. But if someone touches your body, you say, "I have been touched" — you do have the I-sense. in the body. Thus, you conclude that I, the subject, is this physical body. If the body is tall, I am tall; if the body is short, I am short; dark, I am dark; slim, I am slim; fat, I am fat. Above my head or beyond the tip of my nose I do not exist. Since I take this body and myself as identical, I conclude that all limitations that belong to the body belong to me. That I am mortal is a natural conclusion, because when the body is born, I am born, and when it goes, I go. This conclusion is not as valid as you think; in fact, it is the source of all your problems.

Here begins the real inquiry. We probe this notion of the body being the Self, and prove its falsity. The knower is the subject, I, and anything that is known is the object, this. The question is asked, "Is this physical body known or not?" When one says, "I am tall", zis the tall, physical body known or not? If it were not known, the speaker could not say, "I am tall." If the body is known, the body is only an object, not the subject, I.

When, you see a tall building, you know that you are distinct from the building, for the seer is always distinct from the seen; the knower is always distinct from the known. This physical body is an object of your perception. You are aware of this physical body just as you are aware of any other body. You cannot therefore be the body which is an object of your knowledge; you must be someone who is distinct from the body, even though associated with it. If you, the subject, are not the body, then who are you?

Are You the Sense Organs?

You may say you are the sense organs, the organs of

perception. Through them you hear, touch, see, taste, and smell the objects of the world. One may say, "Because my eyes are bright, I am bright; if my eyes are blind, I am blind; if dull, I am dull. Therefore, I am the eyes." But are you not the knower of the eyes? The condition of the eyes is known to you. The subject, the knower, must be distinct from the known, the sense organs. You can rightly say that you are the knower of the deafness of your ears, the blindness of your eyes, or the congestion in your nose, but you are not the deaf ears, the blind eyes, or the blocked nose.

If you are not the sense organs, who are you? Who is the knower?

Are You the Mind?

You may think, "I am the mind." It is true that you operate the sense organs with the mind, gathering experiences. If the mind is not there, the sense organs cannot make you see, hear, or taste. If the mind is restless, you are restless; if it is quiet, you are quiet; if sad, you are sad; if angry, you are angry. Nobody says, "My mind is restless but I am fine."

You say you are restless because you take the mental condition of restlessness as yourself. But you *know* the restless mind; it is an object of your knowledge, and you, the knower, are distinct from it. Therefore you are not the mind.

Who, then, are you?

Are You the Intellect?

You cannot name your profession and say, " I am a lawyer." You were not born a lawyer. You went to school, studied, and became a lawyer. You are a lawyer as a result of your intellectual achievement; you know law just as you know the mind and its conditions. You are the knower, not the object of your knowledge.

Neither are you memory, for memories also are gathered and recalled by you who are aware of memories. You cannot say, "I am Gupta," because it is a name given to you, used in records. Even your friends have different names for you. By changing your name they do not change you; you are the same person who bears different names.

The question still remains, "Who are you?"

Are You Ignorance?

Perhaps you will now say, "Since I am not the body, sense organs, emotions, or knowledge, I must be the pure ignorance that obtains in deep sleep when all knowledge is absent." The Vedas say that in sleep *Andhah anandho bhavati:* the blind is no longer blind." Neither is one, who can see, aware that he is not blind. In deep sleep neither the blind person nor the sighted one knows even the condition of his or her own eyes and yet, in the morning, each wakes up and says, "I slept well." For one to say, "I slept well," the I must have been there even though the knowledge of everything in this world was absent. Since knowledge was absent and yet you remain, you may conclude, "I am nothing, I am ignorance."

But if you were that ignorance, you could not say, "I slept well." This means that you do seem to know at least that you were there. If I ask,"Do you know the Chinese language?" you will say, "I don't know it." If I ask, "How do you know?" you will say,"I know that I don't know." You are aware that you don't know. You also know that you know the fact of your ignorance. You cannot therefore be ignorance.

You Are Awareness

Through this inquiry you are able to conclude that you must be distinct from the body, sense organs, mind, knowledge, memory, and ignorance. You are none of the relative roles, like father, son, etc., because to play a particular role you have to stop playing the others. You are therefore distinct from all of these. You are none of the things you think you are.

You must now say, "I am someone who is aware of my ignorance, my knowledge, my memories, my emotions, my hunger, my sense organs, and my body. All that I hear, see, smell, taste or touch are objects. I am the subject, the aware being, who is aware of all the objects, including the body and the mind,."

Are you the aware being always, or are you the .aware being only in relation to things of which you are aware? Just as you are a seer in relation to objects seen, a hearer in relation to sounds heard, a taster in relation to tastes, you are an aware being only in relation to the objects of which you are aware. Without reference to objects, in relation only to yourself, you are the content of the aware being, the essence of the aware being. That essence can only be Awareness.

This Awareness, I, is limitless and non-dual. Any object can be limited by time, space, or another object; but Awareness, I, is not an object, and so it has no dimension, no shape, no limitation. Since it is limitless, it is non-dual. You are this limitless. This is *sāṅkhya*, the knowledge taught by the Gita. It is not an intellectual knowledge, or a logical theory that we are propounding; here is a valid means of knowledge that makes you see what you really are. Just as no theory or practice is involved in opening your eyes and seeing an object, so it is in this case. The teacher uses logic to make you see what you really are; what is taught is logical; but that you are limitless is neither speculation, nor a concept established by pure logic.

The I that the teacher talks about is Awareness because of which everyone is aware of objects. Awareness can have no form, for if it had a form, it would be a visible object for another awareness. That second awareness, if it were an object, would then be seen by yet another, and so on. This would lead us to the logical absurdity of regress *ad infinitum*. I, Awareness, am formless. There can be no question of bigness or smallness for I, for I am free from any form and I am thus not limited by space. The Gita says, "*Ayam sarvagatah:* This (Self) is all-pervasive." Everything is in that limitless Awareness. I am Awareness, you are Awareness; therefore are we not one? Between you-Awareness and I-Awareness, is not there an identity? There can be no second Awareness.

Awareness is Limitless

Think of the moon. If I ask you the distance between the moon and yourself, you may reply that it is some definite number of miles. If I then ask, "What is the distance between space and the moon?" your answer will be that there cannot be any distance between the moon and space because the moon is in space and space is in and through the moon. Distance itself is the space between two objects in space, but between space and space there is no distance.

Similarly, the sun, the sky, the stars all exist within Awareness. Your body exists within Awareness. Space exists within Awareness. There can be no distance. You are Awareness and in Awareness are the stars above; between Awareness and the stars there is no distance. You are Awareness, he is Awareness, she is Awareness, I am Awareness. How many awarenesses are there? There is only one all-pervasive Awareness in which all objects exist.

And this Awareness is not circumscribed by time, because I, Awareness, am aware of time. Anything that is born in time can be destroyed in time; but Awareness, the very basis of time, is beyond the realm of time. Further, because Awareness is formless, it cannot be destroyed by dividing it into parts. Lastly, an object can be destroyed, but Awareness is the subject, the basis of everything. Thus all agents of destruction are incapable of destroying I-Awareness. Lord Kṛṣṇa says:

नैनं छिन्दन्ति शस्त्राणि नैनं दहति पावकः ।
न चैनं क्लेदयन्त्यापो न शोषयति मारुतः ॥ २–२३ ॥

अच्छेद्योऽयमदाह्योऽयमक्लेद्योऽशोष्य एव च ।
नित्यः सर्वगतः स्थाणुरचलोऽयं सनातनः ॥ २–२४ ॥

Nainaṁ chindanti śastrāṇi nainaṁ dahati pāvakaḥ
Na cainaṁ kledayantyāpo na śoṣayati mārutaḥ (II:23)

Acchedyo'yamadāhyo'yamakledyo'śoṣya eva ca
Nityassarvagatassthāṇuracalo'yaṁ'sanātanaḥ (II:24)

Weapons cannot cut it; fire cannot burn it; water cannot wet it; even wind cannot dry it. It is not subject to being cut, burned, wet or dried. It is beyond time, all-pervasive, immovable, and immutable.

In sleep, neither time nor space, nor the mind which objectifies the world, exists; but I exist in and through waking, dream, and sleep. Therefore I am not circumscribed by space or time; I am *sarvagata,* all-pervasive, and *nitya,* free from the limitation of time.

In Awareness are space and time, and in time-space alone is the whole creation. Therefore, I am free from all limitations. Talking about Awareness, Lord Kṛṣṇa says:

अव्यक्तोऽयमचिन्त्योऽयमविकार्योऽयमुच्यते ।
तस्मादेवं विदित्वैनं नानुशोचितुमर्हसि ॥ २-२५ ॥

Avyakto'yamacintyo'yamavikāryo'yamucyate
Tasmādevaṁ viditvainaṁ nānuśocitumarhasi (II:25)

This is not manifest (cannot be perceived), nor can this be thought of (as one thinks of an object); not subject to mutation either (because it is not born). Therefore, knowing this Awareness to be thus, you have no cause for grief.

If one takes oneself to be the physical body, reasons for grief are countless, for the physical body has countless limitations. It has no capacity to fly like a bird; it does not have a dog's sense of smell nor the sonar system of a bat; thus it is limited. Things that you have not yet acquired and the things that you have already lost number in the millions, which is reason enough for you to have a long face. All this is due to the wrong conclusion: "I am the physical body, I am mortal."

Your fear of mortality is illegitimate because you are not limited by time or space; you are Awareness, and in you lies the very concept of time and space. That you feel you are ignorant is also illegitimate, for you are Awareness in which all forms of knowledge exist. Any sorrow that you entertain is without a basis, for you are full and complete; you are limitless. Thus Lord Kṛṣṇa says to Arjuna, "*Aśocyānanvaśocastvaṁ*: You are grieved over things that do not deserve grief."

6
You Are Happiness

In the second chapter Lord Kṛṣṇa begins to teach Arjuna *sāṅkhya*, the knowledge of the Self. The Self, *ātmā*, is free from any form of limitation. Since one does not realise its limitlessness, it is perceived wrongly. One takes oneself to be a being limited in time and place, having limited knowledge, and suffering the limitation of sorrow. These feelings of limitation are innate in every human being. We all go about doing things to gain freedom from limitation. All the striving in life is the manifestation of this erroneous conclusion that one is limited. Lord Kṛṣṇa knows that Arjuna too considers himself to be a limited being. He therefore imparts to him the knowledge that removes this error.

Limitation Is Not Real

You conclude that you are mortal, that you are ignorant and sorrowful, because you take yourself to be someone other than what you really are. If you were, by nature, limited, you would not strive against limitation, because what is natural is naturally acceptable. The fact that you strive against mortality, sorrow, and ignorance shows that these are not acceptable to you, because they are against your nature. You are not mortal. You are not your physical body.

Your physical body is an object known to you; calling this object "I" is an error. Of the thousands of houses in the city, you have a particular relationship with one that you call your own; similarly, you have a special relationship with one particular body that you call yours. To conclude that you are the body, however, is as wrong as concluding that you are the house.

You are aware of your physical body; similarly, of your hunger, thirst, thoughts, knowledge, memories, mind — quiet or restless — and ignorance. They are objects of your awareness. You are the knower, distinct from anything that in known. Your nature is simple Awareness, *cit.*

The Nature of Awareness

This I, Awareness, has no form; it is not confined here or elsewhere. Just as there is no inside or outside in space, there is no inside or outside in Awareness. All descriptions of location's in space are only relative. You may say that in relation to the walls of a room you are inside and the others are outside. Now if you think in terms of space, you will say that you, the others, the walls themselves, the planets — in fact, the whole universe — are in space. Similarly, all objects known — including one's own body — are within Awareness. An object can be beyond your thought, but it cannot be beyond the scope of Awareness. You mistake thought to be Awareness, and conclude that when you think of an object, it alone is in Awareness, because it alone is in your thought. This unfortunate conclusion can be proved wrong by shifting one's focus from thought to Awareness. From this perspective one recognizes that the object, the thinker, and the thought are all in a single, indivisible Awareness.

Time exists only in Awareness. In sleep or in a moment of joy you are not aware of time; that moment when time is resolved is eternity, timelessness. People commonly refer to the eternal as something that exists continuously for a long period of time; but eternity cannot be a length ot time, because time does not encompass eternity. A mountain may have existed for a very long time, but it is not eternal, for you can see time's effect on it. Anything that exists in time must undergo change. That which is eternal can only be that which remains unaffected by time. Awareness is the very basis of the concepts of time and space. Time comes and goes; Awareness timelessly exists. I-Awareness is beyond time and hence not subject to death. Therefore, Lord Kṛṣṇa says, killing or causing others to be killed is totally immaterial to:

वेदाविनाशिनं नित्यं य एनमजमव्ययम् ॥ २-२१ ॥

Vedāvināśinaṁ nityaṁ ya enamajamavyayaṁ (II:21)

The one who knows this Self to be indestructible , eternal, unborn, and not subject to decline

Awareness is free from time, for it has neither birth nor death. It exists *always* as the basis of every thought. Before a thought is born, there is Awareness; while the thought exists, Awareness does, but even when the thought is gone, Awareness still remains. The following illustration makes this easy to understand. Before the wave is born, there is water; as long as the wave remains, water also remains, but even when the wave is gone, water still remains; the wave has simply resolved itself into water. In the same manner, thoughts arise, exist and resolve themselves into awareness.

The space-time framework exists in Awareness. Awareness cannot come and go because it is beyond time; it always exists. So *cit* is called *sat,* existence. I, Awareness, has no boundary in space or time; it is free from all limitations.

Dispelling the Notion of Limitation

It is now clear that any sense of limitation is only an erroneous notion, based on identification with the body. You cannot weep for your death, because you are Awareness, which is not bound by time. You cannot weep for your ignorance, because you are Awareness, in which all knowledge exists. Your body cannot limit you; your mind and sense organs do not limit you; objects such as the sea, the stars, the sky, or the laughter on the face of a person do not limit you; for all these are objects of your Awareness. You are limited only by the notion that you are the body: a notion that causes you to go about doing things so that you can become limitless.

Since ignorance is the problem, the solution lies in knowing, not in doing. There is only one I, *ātmā,* which is limitless, and about which you are confused. You will not, and need not, find another *ātmā.* This confusion is resolved by the teaching which removes your ignorance of *ātmā.* The removal of that ignorance is *sāṅkhya.*

A New Problem

A new problem may now arise. You may say that in spite of

having heard that the Self is limitless Awareness, you still feel limited, and all the more sad because you know that *ātmā* is beyond sadness. Knowledge of the Self appears only to accentuate your feeling of sadness, for you do not seem to enjoy the limitlessness that is said to be your nature. To resolve this new problem, we must first analyse the nature of happiness.

The State of Man

Happiness and sorrow, *sukha* and *duhkha,* come and go unpredictably in any person's life, with sorrow reigning longer than happiness. Everybody does pick up happiness now and then — even the most unhappy person laughs helplessly at a slapstick joke. That momentary *sukha,* gained once in a while, keeps one going, for it gives one hope that a future day will be happier; otherwise, one would commit suicide. Where should we look for more of that happiness?

Is Happiness an Object?

Among the countless objects in the world, is there an object called happiness? You can make someone happy by giving him or her a piece of sweet, but you cannot say that the object is happiness. For a naturopath a cup of half-cooked, unsalted bitter gourd is happiness; but for some others nothing could be more bitter. For one who loves rich sweet food, a heavy dessert is happiness but for one who does not like such food, it is only an invitation to indigestion. No particular object can be called happiness, for no single object can provide happiness to everyone.

Neither can you say that happiness is a quality of an object, as colour is a quality of a lotus. There is no object with happiness as its quality, for if such an object existed, everyone would become happy by having that object. Sugar or salt tastes the same to everyone, but no object gives the same taste of happiness to all.

Still, people do seem to pick up happiness from contact with objects. If that happiness does not lie in the objects, where is it?

Is Happiness within Me?

If happiness lies within you, is it in your liver, intestines, heart, kidneys, or pancreas? It is, of course, absurd to say that any one of these internal organs is happiness, or that they secrete happiness. Neither are your sense organs a source of happiness, for if they were, you would always be happy, because these organs are always in your body. Neither can one say that thoughts are the source of happiness, for often thoughts are a source of great sorrow.

You Are Happiness

If happiness is neither inside nor outside you, where is it? Only one possibility remains: the Self — because of which you are aware of your body , your emotions, your thoughts, and all the objects of the world— must be the source of happiness.

If you are happiness, why is it that you seem to become happy only when you come in contact with certain people, situations, or objects? If you analyse what happens in a given moment of happiness, you will discover that contact with anything that you like creates in you a pleased mind. When you desire something, the mind is restless; when the desired object is gained, the restlessness is resolved and the mind is satisfied. The happiness you discover is in this satisfied, pleased mind, not in any object. People, situations, and objects that can bring about in you a pleased mind are the ones you love. Not all objects can do this; because of your background, values, and upbringing, only certain objects and individuals please you. But the happiness that you feel never comes from objects or people, however dear they may be. Happiness is manifest only in a satisfied mind, a mind that desires nothing, because the Self is the source of happiness. The joy that you feel when you see something beautiful or hear a pleasing song is an expression of your own nature — a speck of the limitless happiness that you are.

Sleep, a State of Happiness

The experience of sleep confirms that your nature is indeed happiness; everyone likes to sleep and is reluctant to get up, because sleep is a happy experience, a respite from having to carry the burdens that we do during the day. There is a total absence of sorrow in sleep, because all differences are resolved under the blanket of sleep. All forms of duality vanish; there is no difference between the sleep of a king and that of a beggar. In the total absence of all else, you are with yourself alone. The happiness that you experience is yourself.

Happiness is the Absence of Desires

Whenever your mind does not long for anything, you are happy. In the interval between the fulfilment of one desire and the cropping up of the next, you are happy. Why do you sing in the shower? You don't do it to please yourself or anyone else; you do it simply because you are happy. At that time, the mind does not long for anything; all the window dressings, the masks you wear for people, are removed with your clothes - you are with yourself. Your singing is an expression of the happiness felt by a mind that rests in the Self.

A person who understands that the Self is the source of all happiness will be free from all desires. In the last section of the second chapter, the Lord describes such a person to Arjuna, saying:

प्रजहाति यदा कामान्सर्वान्पार्थ मनोगतान् ।
आत्मन्येवात्मना तुष्टः स्थितप्रज्ञस्तदोच्यते ॥ २–५५ ॥

Prajahāti yadā kāmānsarvānpārtha manogatān
Atmanyevātmanā tuṣṭaḥ sthitaprajñastadocyate (II:55)

When one completely renounces all the desires entertained by the mind, satisfied in the Self, by the Self, one is called a person of steady wisdom.

Just as fire is hot not because of any reason but by nature, so a wise man is happy not because of any reason, but because happiness is his nature. Since a wise man knows that the Self is the source of happiness, he requires nothing; by this knowledge, he casts away all desires.

Neither a ripple nor a breaker can add to the greatness of

the ocean; each is only a fleeting expression of its greatness. The ocean remains unaffected even when these forms disappear. When you gain an object of your desire, the happiness that you experience is like a wave in the ocean. It is only a momentary expression of the happiness that is yourself; and when it comes to an end, the fullness, *ānanda*, that you are, remains unchanged. The one who recognizes that the Self is *sat-cit-ānanda* — existence, Awareness, and fullness — is wise. That person is called *sthitaprajña,* well-rooted in wisdom.

In a later verse, the wise person is likened to the ocean into which rivers flow:

आपूर्यमाणमचलप्रतिष्ठं
समुद्रमापः प्रविशन्ति यद्वत् ।
तद्वत्कामा यं प्रविशन्ति सर्वे
स शान्तिमाप्नोति न कामकामी ॥ २–७० ॥

Āpūryamāṇamacalapratiṣṭhaṁ
samudramāpaḥ praviśanti yadvat
Tadvatkāmā yaṁ praviśanti sarve
sa śāntimāpnoti na kāmakāmī (II:70)

The one into whom all desires enter, as waters flow into the ocean, which remains unchanged and ever full, that one gains peace, and not the one who desires objects.

The ocean remains ever the same; it does not flood when rivers pour water into it, nor is it diminshed when rivers cease to flow in. The ocean does not depend on any other source of water; all waters spring only from the ocean.

Like the ocean, the wise man's heart is ever full. Whether or not the world cares for him, whether or not he gets what he wants, he is happy; his fullness does not depend on the arrival or departure of anything. In contrast, a person who depends upon objects in order to be happy will be elated by getting what he or she wants, and depressed by not getting it. This sort of person is like a pond that dries up if the rains do not come, and overflows when it is filled to the brim by one shower.

Continuing his description of a wise person, Lord Kṛṣṇa says:

विहाय कामान्यः सर्वान्पुमांश्चरति निःस्पृहः ।
निर्ममो निरहङ्कारः स शान्तिमधिगच्छति ॥ २-७१ ॥

Vihāya kāmānyassarvān pumāmścarati nisspṛhaḥ
Nirmamo nirahankāraḥ sa 'sāntimadhigacchati (II:71)

Having given up all desires, the man who moves about without attachment, who has no thought of "I" or "my", gains peace.

A wise person does not depend upon anything for happiness, and so lives in the world without fear or attachment, moving about as freely as the air. Such a person can enter or leave any situation without any problem. Lord Kṛṣṇa himself was like this: always laughing, involved in all events, but not caught up in them.

The Lord continues:

एषा ब्राह्मी स्थितिः पार्थ नैनां प्राप्य विमुह्यति ।
स्थित्वास्यामन्तकालेऽपि ब्रह्मनिर्वाणमृच्छति ॥ २-७२ ॥

Eṣā brāhmī sthitiḥ pārtha naināṃ prāpya vịmuhyati
Sthitvāsyāmantakāle'pi brahmanirvāṇamṛchhati (II:72)

Having attained this *brāhmī* state, the limitless, O Arjuna, one is no longer deluded. Having been established in that state, even if only at the end of one's life, one attains oneness with brahman, the limitless.

The space in a small pot is the same as in a large pot; both are limitless space. The pot space that understands that it is only apparently limited by the walls of the pot because even the pot is within space, will realise that it is identical with limitless space, and will no longer feel limited. This knowledge is called here the *brāhmī* state, a state that is Brahman, limitlessness. It is not a state of experience; it is the vision of the mind brought about by the knowledge that one is free from all limitation.

Once gained, knowledge cannot be lost, for ignorance that has been removed cannot return. A person who has gained knowledge of Self will never again be deluded. There can be no feeling of inferiority for one who recognizes oneself as fullness, for nothing can be compared to fullness. Even God is not superior to one who knows oneself to be the one Awareness, because of which God is aware of His omniscience and the individual is aware of his or her limited knowledge. In Awareness there is no distinction. This vision is *sāṅkhya*.

7
Karma Yoga

In the second chapter of the Gita, *sāṅkhya*, the knowledge of oneself, is unfolded. The self is free from death and free from any form of limitation whatsoever. Yet, one wants to be free. Through knowledge one realises that what is sought is the very nature of the seeker, that happiness is not something to be gained, for it is already contained in oneself. Thus, understanding oneself to be happiness, one gives up the desire to become happy. Lord Kṛṣṇa concludes the chapter by saying that the person from whom all desires have gone, who is free from attachment, gains tranquillity.

Arjuna's Confusion

There is a world of difference between what Lord Kṛṣṇa means by these words and Arjuna's understanding of them. The wise man knows that he is happiness, and so grows out of the desire to become happy by gaining objects; his happiness does not depend on the presence or absence of things. Arjuna, however, understands this to mean that one must give up desires in order to be happy. He is, as it were, saying to the Lord, "O Lord, I want to be happy. Now I see that the objects of the world do not have the happiness that I seek. If, as you say, happiness is myself, should I not turn my back on the world and seek happiness within myself? Should I not leave the world to those who are interested in it and go to a quiet place to meditate and discover the happiness that I am?"

Arjuna feels that withdrawing from the world is the way to gain happiness. However, Lord Kṛṣṇa tells him that he must act, saying:

हतो वा प्राप्स्यसि स्वर्गं जित्वा वा भोक्ष्यसे महीम् ।
तस्मादुत्तिष्ठ कौन्तेय युद्धाय कृतनिश्चयः ॥ २–३७ ॥

Hato vā prāpsyasi svargaṁ jitvā vā bhokṣyase mahīm
Tasmāduttiṣṭha kaunteya yuddhāya kṛtaniścayaḥ (II:37)

If you are killed, you will gain heaven; if you win, you will enjoy the earth. Therefore O son of Kunti, arise, determined to fight.

Arjuna wonders which choice is better - fighting or quitting the battle. He therefore asks a question:

ज्यायसी चेत्कर्मणस्ते मता बुद्धिर्जनार्दन ।
तत्किं कर्मणि घोरे मां नियोजयसि केशव ॥ ३-१ ॥

Jyāyasī cetkarmaṇaste matā buddhirjanārdana
Tatkiṁ karmaṇi ghore māṁ niyojayasi keśava (III:1)

If it is your conclusion that knowledge is superior to action, O Janārdana,[1] why do you direct me to do this horrible deed, O Keśava?[2]

By these words Arjuna seems to say, "O Lord, you seem to be confusing me. You praise knowledge highly. You compare the wise man to the ocean, saying that his heart is ever full because he does not depend upon anything for his joy. At the same time, you ask me to take up weapons and fight. I have said that I want only śreyas, and yet you ask me to perform action. Why do you ask me to fight the battle? If you mean that knowledge is good for some and action for others your instruction would be understandable, but you seem to ask me to pursue both. How can I fight in the battlefield and still pursue knowledge? If knowledge is superior to action, why do you lead me into this act of fighting?"

व्यामिश्रेणेव वाक्येन बुद्धिं मोहयसीव मे ।
तदेकं वद निश्चित्य येन श्रेयोऽहमाप्नुयाम् ॥ ३-२ ॥

Vyāmiśreṇeva vākyena buddhiṁ mohayasīva me
Tadekaṁ vada niścitya yena śreyo'hamāpnuyāṁ (III:2)

1&2. Names of Lord Kṛṣṇa. Janārdana means the one who protects people and Keśva means the killer of the demon Keśi.

You confuse my mind with words that are seemingly confusing. Tell me definitely the one means by which I may gain *sreyas.*

Arjuna understands that knowledge and action are opposed to each other. They cannot be simultaneously pursued by the same person. Therefore he requests the Lord to tell him the one thing that he should pursue to attain *śreyas.*

Even though Arjuna is asking Lord Kṛṣṇa to tell him which to pursue - knowledge or action - he thinks that action can only bring about bondage, not freedom. He might have reasoned like this: "Any action I perform is only for a result, and because I expect a result, I am going to be bound by the action. The very expectation will make me judge the result - and myself — as a failure or a success. This unavoidable sense of success or failure can only create in me mental agitation. I shall never find peace as long as I am engaged in action.

"However, if I don't perform action there will be no expectation of results, no judgement of myself as a failure or a success, no reaction of depression or elation. Why should I act and cause a chain of reactions? I would rather give up all action, retire to a quiet place, and contemplate. O Lord, you have already taught me that I am *sat-cit-ānanda,* existence, knowledge, fullness. To accept this teaching, one must live a life of contemplation, free from duties.

"However, you are asking me to perform action. This can only lead to the chain of expectations, results, judgements, reactions, problems. There will be no opportunity to contemplate upon myself or God. I do not understand why you want me to engage in action. Please decide and tell me definitely which is right for me, action or renunciation."

The Problem of Likes and Dislikes

Everyone lives in a private world conditioned by society, culture, religion, parents and teachers. As a result of these influences each person has very definite likes and dislikes. One likes objects possession of which, one feels, will make one happy. One dislikes objects in the presence of which one will be unhappy. There are also objects and beings to which one is indifferent, because their presence or absence does create happiness or unhappiness.

One does not see the objects of the world as they are, but

sees them as they appear to the mind which has peculiar likes and dislikes. One may have a liking for jasmine and a dislike for rose, though no sin is committed by the rose. Rose and jasmine are different, to be sure, but neither is superior to the other. The more sensitive a person is, the more particular these likes and dislikes become. You may see a red rose and say, "I love rose, but I wish this one were white." A sensitive and a cultured person has a preference in everything, even in the different shades of one colour. Having preferences is not in itself a problem, but if one likes or dislikes a certain shade, one does not see that shade as it is. Thus all the objects of the world are coloured by definite likes and dislikes, and each person lives not in the public world, the objective world, but in a private world of fantasy and fancy.

All one's pursuits are governed by these likes and dislikes. One thinks one will be happier, more comfortable, by acquiring the objects one likes and getting rid of objects one dislikes. A person can be made uncomfortable by many small things, beginning with his or her own gray hair. The desire to be happy drives one to acquire and reject according to one's likes and dislikes. One's happiness is, therefore, uncertain because it depends on the success of one's pursuit; and it is made even more uncertain by the fact that one's likes and dislikes are not constant. An object of love today can become an object of hate tomorrow. An object of dislike can become an object of liking; an object to which one is indifferent can become an object of love in future.

If one feels cheated in this world, it is not because of the objective world, but because of one's own fancies. Even God cannot make a person happy when he or she lives in a private world of likes and dislikes. Until those likes and dislikes are neutralized, one cannot be objective about the world, and until one is objective, one suffers needlessly.

How can one neutralise likes and dislikes? We are generally told to give up likes and dislikes, but we cannot do that because they are not like a shirt or a hat that can be removed. We do not only *have* likes and dislikes; we *have a value* for them; likes and dislikes are the very fabric of our personalities. We cannot remove likes and dislikes like weeds in a garden

Even when you perform an action prompted by your likes

or dislikes, if you do not react to the result when it comes, your likes or dislikes are neutralised. The result of an action is rarely in accordance with your expectations. If it is better than what you anticipated, you think you are successful and you feel elated. If you get less than what you expected, you call yourself a failure. But if you take the results objectively, your like or dislike cannot create any feeling of success or failure in you. Likes and dislikes thus become defused, not capable of causing any unhappiness.

Likes and Dislikes : Obstacles to Knowledge

For a person who, like Arjuna, wants only the knowledge that brings freedom from sorrow, ignorance, and mortality, likes and dislikes create another problem: a mind ruled by likes and dislikes cannot abide in knowledge. A person with likes and dislikes may see what is being said when the teacher says, "You are *sat-cit-ānanda,*" because the mind is held in attention and therefore it is relatively free; the mind has become a learning mind with which likes and dislikes do not interfere. But it is only by the glory of the teaching that one is able to appreciate what is taught. Those moments of learning in which one glimpses one's real Self are isolated from one's personality. Later, away from the teacher and the teaching, these glimpses vanish and what remains is only a personality ruled as before by likes and dislikes. The momentary experience may even seem to be a hypnotic spell.

One cannot own up to the teaching that one is limitlessness and happiness until likes and dislikes are neutralised. Arjuna is afraid of performing action neither because of action, nor even because of results. He is afraid of his reaction to the results, and because of this fear he wants to renounce action. Arjuna does not understand that performing action with a change of attitude is the way to neutralise likes and dislikes and gain a relatively free mind with which to appreciate the teaching and therefore he thinks that Lord Kṛṣṇa's advice to engage in action is contradictory to his praise of knowledge. In reply the Lord says:

लोकेऽस्मिन्द्विविधा निष्ठा पुरा प्रोक्ता मयानघ ।
ज्ञानयोगेन साङ्ख्यानां कर्मयोगेन योगिनाम् ॥ ३-३ ॥

Loke'smindvividhā niṣṭhā purā proktā mayānagha
Jñānayogena sāṅkhyānāṁ karmayogena yogināṁ (III: 3)

O sinless one, in this world the twofold pursuit was taught by Me at the beginning of creation: pursuit of knowledge for the contemplative ones, and performance of action for the active ones.

There are two ways of living: one is the life of renunciation while seeking knowledge, and the other is the life of action seeking the same knowledge. Action is involved in one mode and not in the other, but what is sought in both is only freedom, through knowledge.

How to decide which mode one should adopt?

If you are already contemplative, the decision is clear - you are fit for the contemplative life. But no one can ask someone to be contemplative, just as no one can ask someone to appreciate the beauty of a flower or love another person. These capacities cannot be made to order; they must be discovered. You cannot adopt a contemplative life by merely giving up possessions. You will only deny yourself whatever you had. and perhaps become lazy as well. A contemplative attitude is natural, but it can be discovered only if likes and dislikes do not have a hold over you. As long as likes and dislikes hold sway over you, you cannot be contemplative.

Imagine that you are in a quiet place near a forested mountain with a quiet river flowing by, flowers all around, birds singing. The world is beautiful; you don't seem to desire anything; you have settled accounts with the world for the time being, and you feel very happy. It is this same happy person who used to answer a simple "How do you do?" with a million complaints. How have all those complaints disappeared? When you saw the mountain, you didn't want it to be different; had you desired it to have an icy peak, you would not have been as happy as you are. The mind has accepted everything as it is; it doesn't want the river to flow faster or slower, or the sky to be bluer or the birds more musical. You yourself do not want to be different. Had you felt the need for someone to talk to, the beauty would have been lost. At that moment, all your likes and dislikes are resolved. You are peaceful and happy. This is the state of mind conducive to contemplation.

The objective world does not create any problem for you. Problems are caused only by a mind dominated by likes and dislikes. If you have a contemplative mind, you can defuse the likes and dislikes by being aware that they belong to the mind, and that you are different from the mind. This is why Lord Kṛṣṇa first gives Arjuna the knowledge of the nature of the Self. Now the Lord presents a method of neutralising the likes and dislikes by cultivating a particular attitude towards action and its result. This method is meant to help those who, like Arjuna, have not discovered in themselves a contemplative mind because of the pull of their likes and dislikes. The method is called *karma yoga.*

Giving up Action is Not Possible

Action binds a person and perpetuates bondage only if one's attitude is not right. When Arjuna asks Lord Kṛṣṇa, "Why are you making me engage in this cruel action?" the Lord makes it clear that action can never be given up entirely:

न हि कश्चित्क्षणमपि जातु तिष्ठत्यकर्मकृत् ॥ ३–५ ॥

शरीरयात्रापि च ते न प्रसिद्ध्येदकर्मणः ॥ ३–८ ॥

Na hi kaścitkṣaṇamapi jātu tiṣṭhatyakarmakṛt (III: 5)

Śarīrayātrāpi ca te na prasiddhyedakarmaṇaḥ (III: 8)

Not even for a moment does anyone remain without performing action.

Not even your stay in the physical body can be accomplished without action.

Lord Kṛṣṇa is as though saying to Arjuna, "You may give up the kingdom, you may go to Rishikesh, you may try to lead a contemplative life, but you cannot totally give up action, Arjuna. Even as a *sādhu*, a monk, you have to procure food and masticate it. Your hands and legs, your liver and heart, are all meant only to act; total cessation of all activities, as long as one is alive, is not possible. It is childish to think that action can be given up. In life everyone has roles that must be performed. Even a bolt holding a piston has a role —its role is that it should not move."

To be a renouncer is to be contemplative; it is not to stop all activities and be lazy. Merely stopping all physical activities will not assure a contemplative disposition. You must neutralise the likes and dislikes which buffet your mind.

If you continue to act but do so with a change in attitude towards the results of action, you can neutralise the likes and dislikes and become contemplative. It is for this reason that Lord Kṛṣṇa advises Arjuna, "*Kaunteya, uttistha*: Arjuna, arise!"

Karma Yoga : an Attitude towards Action

In the second chapter, Lord Kṛṣṇa had described to Arjuna the attitude that can defuse one's likes and dislikes while performing action. This attitude is called *karma yoga.*

कर्मण्येवाधिकारस्ते मा फलेषु कदाचन ।
मा कर्मफलहेतुर्भूर्मा ते सङ्गोऽस्त्वकर्मणि ॥ २–४७ ॥

Karmaṇyevādhikāraste mā phaleṣu kadācana
Mā karmaphalaheturbhūrmā te sango'stvakarmaṇi (II:47)

You have choice over your action but not over the results at any time. Do not (take yourself to) be the author of the results of action; neither be attached to inaction.

Lord Kṛṣṇa begins by drawing Arjuna's attention to a fact: "*Te karmaṇi eva adhikārah, mā phaleṣu:* "Work alone is your privilege, never its results." This sentence has confused many scholars who interpret it to mean that one should perform action without expecting a result. This cannot be the intent of Lord Kṛṣṇa's statement, because it would mean that he would teach Arjuna without expecting him to understand. No one performs action without expecting some result.

What then does the statement mean?

The statement is very clear: you have a choice in your action, but never in the results. The result is determined the moment the action is performed. You cannot avoid *karmaphala*, the fruit of action. One cannot jump out of a window and expect the result, falling, not to happen, nor can one expect gravity to pull one's body at a rate less than 32 feet per second per second! The results of action are governed by laws that are not under our control.

We find ourselves in a world governed by laws that are not created by anyone here. We are born according to laws, and the reaping of results is also according to laws. The relationship between an action and its results is governed by the laws of nature, which we can attempt to understand but never change.

The author of these laws is the one we call God or, in Sanskrit, *īśvara*. It is by His laws that I get a particular result, not by my choice. Therefore the Lord says, "*Mā karmaphalaheturbhūḥ*: May you not take yourself to be the author of the results of action." The results are produced by laws which are not under our control.

When I undertake to do something, I expect a result, even though I know that the results are not under my control, because I have likes and dislikes which I want to be fulfilled. This expectation of result, which is natural, is not a problem; the problem lies in our reaction to the results when they come. The meaning of the verse is: perform action expecting results; act so that you can achieve what you desire; plan and execute your work; but if the result is totally contrary to your expectations in spite of all your wishing and willing, don't react and call yourself a failure.

It is possible to prevent such a reaction if you enjoy an attitude born of an understanding of the nature of actions and their results. An action produces a result that is inherent in the action itself. One cannot expect what is not contained in the action. You are not the maker of laws that govern the results of actions, nor do you know all the laws that come into play to yield a result; but you do know that things function according to laws and that there is a harmony in the functioning of the universe. For any action, a proper result always accrues according to the laws.

You don't feel grateful to the banker or the postman when you get the money sent by your son every month. They are only instruments who convey the money to you from your son who is your benefactor. Likewise, laws are only instruments of the Lord who gives you the result of action. Even when you read these words, the reading takes place according to His laws. When you understand this fact, you develop a special attitude: you appreciate that the result of every action comes from the Lord.

Prasāda Buddhi : Graceful Acceptance

What is one's attitude towards an object received after worship at a temple or communion in a church? Such an object is viewed as coming from the Lord, and so it is accepted differently from the same object acquired in some other way. Let us consider a flower, a marigold. Normally when someone picks a marigold from the garden, he or she smells it and enjoys the fragrance. But there is a difference in one's response to the same flower, if it is received after having been offered to the Lord at the altar in the house. An Indian would bring it to his or her eyes, a gesture reserved for objects that are very sacred. What prompted this change of attitude? The flower that has been offered at the altar is now a blessing from the Lord and not merely a fragrant flower. The same attitude of reverence is felt towards any object that you receive in a temple or a church, be it ash, water, sugar crystal or a piece of bread. What you do with the object varies — you apply the ash on your forehead while you eat the sugar — but your attitude towards each is the same. You are not concerned with who gave you the object or how much you received. For you, it is *prasāda*, a blessing from the Lord,. and that is enough. The attitude that you show towards *prasāda* is *prasāda buddhi,* a graceful acceptance of whatever comes with reverence.

Success and failure are only relative. Suppose in a joint venture you expect 50 per cent profit and your partner expects only 15 per cent. If the profit turns out to be 20 per cent you will be disappointed, while your partner will be happy. Since the expectations are different, the same result is seen differently. So too by a change of attitude, a simple flower gains the special status of *prasāda*. In the same way if you accept the result of your action as *prasāda*, though the tangible result remains the same, your vision of the result is changed. With this in view, the Lord tells Arjuna, "*Mā te saṅgo'-stvakarmaṇi:* Do not be inclined to inaction." The Lord advises Arjuna not to run away from the battle but to engage in action; and when the result comes, to regard it as *prasāda.*

You perform an action prompted by desire. You appreciate the fact that the result comes from the Lord, that is, it is shaped according to His laws. The result is thus *prasāda* from the Lord. When you have this attitude, you accept any result with an open mind, without apprehension, as you accept any *prasāda.* Cultivating *prasāda buddhi* towards the result of actions is *karma yoga.* With a limited mind you can only estimate what the result will be, but you appreciate that the result will always be true to the action; that you will not be deceived. You don't react, whether or not the results are according to your expectations, because those results are *prasāda* from the Lord.

Prasāda means absence of sorrow. Once a situation is accepted as *prasāda*, your mind enjoys *prasannatā*, cheerfulness. This cheerfulness is a blessing, because when it is present, your likes and dislikes are no longer capable of creating any reaction in your mind. When you obtain a result which is not what you expected, be it success or failure, your likes and dislikes are neutralised if you accept it as *prasāda.*

Īsvarārpaṇa Buddhi : Offering Action to the Lord

There is another attitude by which you can defuse the effects of the likes and dislikes on your personality. This attitude is based on an appreciation of the Lord not just when the results of action are gained, but even before you begin your action.

There are two important defining sentences of *karma yoga* in the Gita. One, *samatvaṁ yoga ucyatė* - sameness (of mind) is *yoga.* The other, *yogaḥ karmasu kauśalam* — the right choice *(kauśalam)* in respect of action is yoga. *Samatvaṁ* is possible only with reference to one's response to the results of action. *Prasāda buddhi* grants the attitude to have the sameness of mind to the various results of action. The choice with reference to action is to go by right and wrong as determined by scriptures even if the choice is against one's personal likes and dislikes.

Whatever activity you are engaged in, whether or not it was induced by your own likes and dislikes, you see that every action is controlled by the laws that were created by the Lord. If I am a great singer, I see the fact that I did not come into this world and acquire my voice - I was born with it. I thank Him for providing me with this voice; the very act of singing becomes a thanksgiving to the Lord. At every turn I see His hands, His gifts. I make my performance an offering to Him. The Lord says later in the Gita that any action can be an offering to the Lord, for He is everything. A deep understanding can make one hold this attitude of *īśvarārpaṇa buddhi*, an attitude of offering all to the Lord, towards any activity one engages in, thus steadying the mind against the influence of likes and dislikes.

If you cannot have an attitude of dedication while you perform an action, at least when the result comes accept it as *prasāda* from the Lord. By either of the attitudes, likes and dislikes are neutralised. By *īsvarārpaṇa buddhi*, likes and dislikes are no longer the motivation of action; by *prasāda buddhi* they are no longer a standard for judging the results and yourself.

This is *karma yoga.* Appreciate the fact that the result of your action follows the Creator's laws, which never fail. Your likes and dislikes cannot toss you between elation and despair if you accept results with *prasāda buddhi.* Your mind, freed from agitation, will become contemplative and the teaching that you are *sat-cit-ānanda* will be as clear as daylight. Therefore you do not have to give up action. Just change your attitude towards action and you will be a different person.

Karma yoga is an often misunderstood term. If, as some think, mere performance of action were *karma yoga*, any business person juggling five phones at one time would be a great *karma yogī*. Some translate the phrase *yogaḥ karmasu kauśalam* as "skill in action is *karma yoga*," but by this criterion even a mercenary killer could be a *karma yogī*. Performing action without expecting the fruit of action is also given as a definition of *karma yoga*, but it is not possible for even a mad man to perform an action without expecting a result. None of these is an accurate definition. The true meaning of *karma yoga* is given by the Lord in one sentence — "*Karmaṇyevādhikāraste mā phaleṣu kadācana:* You have choice only regarding action, not regarding the results thereof." *Karma yoga* is the performance of action with the attitude that all results are shaped by the laws of the Lord; they come from the Lord and so they are gladly accepted.

By cultivating this attitude, one no longer suffers the sorrow and regret that arise when the result of an action falls short of one's expectations. Neither action nor its result creates bondage; for it is the reaction of the mind to the result of an action that creates bondage. To be free from this bondage of feeling limited and sorrowful, one must understand that having chosen an action, one should accept the result as *prasāda*. One who has this attitude is called a *karma yogī*.

The Effect of Karma Yoga

One might naturally ask whether there will be any incentive to act, or any learning as a result of one's experiences, if one accepts all results as coming from the Lord. In fact, only with this attitude can you learn from your experiences. A reacting mind cannot learn, for in its despair, frustration, and helplessness it is unable to see things objectively. There is a common saying that experience is the best teacher. Experience can teach if we assimilate it without reaction; but too often we learn nothing from experience and only regret them.

Learning takes place in those moments when your mind is not reacting — however infrequent such moments may be. You cannot learn when your mind is angry, hateful or jealous; such a state of mind is not receptive. Action is creative and human; reactions such as anger, jealousy, etc., are mechanical. You do not become angry, hateful or jealous by choice. Because of such reactions, you are unable to learn from your experiences. The Lord advises Arjuna to avoid such reactions by recognising that the laws that produce the results of action are not partial to one and cruel to another. The laws that govern the universe are impartial and they never fail. If a result is not according to your expectations, accept it, change your course, and act again. If your action fails, you are not a failure if you learn from your experience. If you accept the result of your actions, as you accept *prasāda* in a temple or a church, and if you perform all your actions as an offering, you will develop a non-reacting mind, a mind capable of learning.

8

Knowledge and Actionlessness

Knowledge Is a Wonder

Lord Kṛṣṇa has taught Arjuna that the Self is indestructible, immortal, unborn, full, and limitless — the source of all happiness; but Arjuna's mind is filled with agitations, caused by conclusions about himself and so he is not able to comprehend the Lord's works fully. To Arjuna's unprepared mind, the knowledge of the Self seems a wonder.

In the second chapter Lord Kṛṣṇa spoke of this wonder:

आश्चर्यवत्पश्यति कश्चिदेन—
माश्चर्यवद्वदति तथैव चान्यः ।
आश्चर्यवच्चैनमन्यः शृणोति
श्रुत्वाप्येनं वेद न चैव कश्चित् ॥ २–२९ ॥

Āścaryavatpaśyati kaścidenaṁ
āścaryavadvadati tathaiva cānyaḥ
Āścaryavaccainamanyassṛṇoti
śrutvāpyenaṁ veda na caiva kaścit (II:29)

Some see this (Self) as a wonder; others speak about it as a wonder. Still others hear this (knowledge) as a wonder. Some, even having heard this, do not understand it.

Some perceive this knowledge as though it is a great wonder because conscious of all their problems and limitations, they cannot imagine that they are happiness that is limitless, beyond time and space Even if one understands this teaching, one still regards it as a wonder because of the mistaken conviction that humankind is by nature sinful and limited. Religions generally make only promises of redemption, saying that if you do this or that, you will be saved; but the Gita says that you need not do anything; you already are *sat-cit-ānanda,* existence, knowledge, fullness. This really is a wonder!

Lord Kṛṣṇa's teaching to Arjuna is not his private, personal understanding of the truth. Truth is not private. Knowledge of oneself, of the world, of God, is not the personal property of anyone. It is as ancient as the creation, handed down through *guru-śiṣya-paramparā,* the teacher-student lineage. A student who is interested in gaining this knowledge goes to a teacher, serves him, and asks him for the knowledge and the *guru* teaches him. Lord Kṛṣṇa describes this tradition in Chapter 4:

तद्विद्धि प्रणिपातेन परिप्रश्नेन सेवया ।
उपदेक्ष्यन्ति ते ज्ञानं ज्ञानिनस्तत्त्वदर्शिनः ॥ ४–३४ ॥

Tadviddhi praṇipātena paripraśnena sevayā
Upadekṣyanti te jñānaṁ jñāninastattvadarśinaḥ (IV: 34)

Know the Self by serving a teacher with an attitude of surrender, by questioning him (about this knowledge) with a desire to know. These wise men, those who see the truth of the Self, will teach you this knowledge.

You cannot hope to discover or intuit this knowledge by yourself; the Self is not an object that you can perceive. You can learn how to divide a cell and split an atom, but how are you going to learn about the one who is learning all this? Someone else has to come and tell you who you really are. For knowledge of yourself, you need a teacher.

The Story of the Missing Tenth Man

The problem of knowing the Self is illustrated by the story of the lost tenth man. Once ten men travelling together came to a river that could only be crossed by swimming. They plunged into it and reached the other bank. Now the leader assembled the group in order to ascertain if all had reached safely and counted them: only nine were there. He counted again and again but every time, he found only nine. The men searched for the missing man frantically up and down the river bank, but their efforts were of no avail — the tenth man was lost. They were all filled with despair. As they sat there weeping, an old man happened to come by and inquired why they were sorrowful. The leader told him about the lost man. The old man closely scrutinised the group and smiled; he instantly understood the problem. "Don't worry," he said, "the tenth man is here; I can produce him right now."

The old man asked all the men to stand in a line. No one knew how he could produce the tenth man by this exercise, but they obeyed because they had *śraddhā*, faith — not blind faith bordering on superstition, but faith pending confirmation. There was, after all, no reason to disbelieve. The old man then asked the leader to step out of the line and count the others. He began to count "One, two..." and so on up to nine. Pointing to the leader, the old man said, "You are the tenth man; you have forgotten to count yourself."

The leader immediately understood; he "gained" the missing man by "realising" that he had been the tenth man all along. How did this realisation take place? By teaching; by the words of the old man the seeker discovered that he was also the sought. As long as he was searching for the missing tenth man he continued to miss him; it could not have occurred to him that he himself might be the tenth man because he had already concluded that the tenth man was lost and had to be searched. With this conclusion, nothing he tried would reveal the tenth man. He could stand on his head, or eat only boiled vegetables for his lifetime, or meditate for hours, but the tenth man would still be missing. He could go to heaven or hell, the tenth man would still be missing. The tenth man could not be found by any action. By his very seeking he was denying the tenth man. Therefore, someone else, a teacher, had to reveal to him the fact that he was the tenth man.

The Need for a Teacher

Similarly, having concluded that you are a mortal, limited and sorrowful, how can you even imagine that you are free from all limitations - that you are the happiness that you are seeking? You cannot. Someone has to teach you, to make you see that your search is futile. You must know who you are in reality; then alone all seeking will end. Therefore, you must go to a teacher who will show you that all that you seek in life is yourself. Using a mirror of words, he will make you see yourself. Thereafter when someone asks when and where you discovered yourself, you will simply smile and be silent. This is not a knowledge that inspires one to be proud and boastful; you will remember how the leader realised what a fool he had been to have been searching for himself. The wise are always modest.

Who Was the First Guru?

You do not question the existence of your great-grandfather even though you may not have seen him; the very fact that you exist proves his existence. That he lived, existed, is thus not a matter of belief. Similarly, the very fact that knowledge of the Self is available now, shows that there must have existed a lineage of teachers and students, transmitting the knowledge generation after generation to the present day. The existence of the knowledge and of the lineage of teachers is, therefore, not a matter of belief, but one of seeing, knowing, understanding.

The question, "Who was the first teacher?", is similar to asking who the first father was. Every father is himself the son of his father, who was also a son of his father. Then who was the first father? You may travel back in time retracing the steps of evolution, but still you cannot determine who the first father was. You can only say that he must have come into being along with creation. The first father is the Lord; so too in the case of the first teacher. Every teacher was once a student and so the first teacher must have been the Lord Himself. Lord Kṛṣṇa describes the beginning of this *guru-śiṣya-paramapará* this way:

इमं विवस्वते योगं प्रोक्तवानहमव्ययम् ।
विवस्वान्मनवे प्राह मनुरिक्ष्वाकवेऽब्रवीत् ॥ ४–१ ॥

एव परम्पराप्राप्तमिमं राजर्षयो विदुः ।
स कालेनेह महता योगो नष्टः परन्तप ॥ ४–२ ॥

Imaṁ vivasvate yogaṁ proktavānahamavyayaṁ
Vivasvānmanave prāha manurikṣvākave'bravīt (IV: 1)

Evaṁ paramparāprāptamimaṁ rājarṣayo viduḥ
Sa kāleneha mahatā yogo naṣṭaḥ parantapa (IV: 2)

I was the one who taught this unchanging *yoga* (knowledge) to Vivasvān (the Sun); he taught it to Manu, and Manu taught it to Ikṣvāku. Thus the kings and wise men knew this (knowledge) handed down in regular succession (of teachers and students). Over a long period of time, O Arjuna, that knowledge has been lost.

Lord Kṛṣṇa thus states: "Though you look upon this knowledge as a wonder, Arjuna, it is an ancient knowledge, as old as creation. It looks strange to you because it is no longer extant because of people like Duryodhana. But it is not lost. Like the sun in a solar eclipse, this knowledge is only covered for the time being."

Praise of Self-knowledge

In praise of this knowledge Lord Kṛṣṇa says:

न हि, ज्ञानेन सदृशं पवित्रमिह विद्यते ॥ ४–३८ ॥

Nahi jñānena sadṛśaṁ pavitramiha vidyate (IV: 38)

There is nothing here (in this world) as purifying as this knowledge

In the Upaniṣads, knowledge of the Self is praised with the words,"*Yena avijñātaṁ vijñātaṁ bhavati:* That by which what is unknown becomes known." How is this possible? It is not that all kinds of knowledge from alchemy to astrophysics will dawn on a person the moment Self-knowledge dawns. The statement of the Upaniṣad only means that a given thing is known as well when the truth of it is known. If water is known, oceans, rivers, lakes, and raindrops are as well known, for water is the truth of all these. Similarly, if the limitless Self is known, everything that exists in the limitless - the entire universe - is as well known, for the limitless is the truth of everything in creation. By this knowledge you gain fullness, total freedom from limitation.

There is nothing equal to this knowledge in releasing you forever from the notion that you are limited and ignorant. Any other branch of knowledge opens up new areas of ignorance: the more you know, the more you realise how much you do not know. An eighth grade student might say, "If an object is tossed up into air, it will come down accelerating at the rate of 32.2 feet per second." The same student, should he or she become a research scholar in physics, would be aware of certain interfering factors and would qualify the statement to say that the acceleration might be that much. This is not a criticism of modern science, but rather an illustration of the indefinite, qualified, relative nature of all objective knowledge. The final word has not yet been said in any discipline of knowledge in the objective world; the present conclusions are always subject to revision in future. This means that ignorance has not gone, for knowledge which is subject to correction is not absolute knowledge.

However *sāṅkhya*, the knowledge of the Self, can for ever release you from ignorance. You are *caitanya*, limitless Awareness; know that, and you are free from all notions of limitation. Hence, there is nothing equal to this knowledge. To gain this, there has to be an abiding mind. Action is the means to neutralise likes and dislikes. creating an abiding mind which is required for learning.

Action and Actionlessness

Lord Kṛṣṇa describes the nature of action and actionlessness:

किं कर्म किमकर्मेति कवयोऽप्यत्र मोहिताः ॥ ४-१६ ॥

Kiṁ karma kimakarmeti kavayo'pyatra mohitāḥ (IV:16)

Even scholars are confused about what is action and what is inaction.

Arjuna might well have wondered what confusion could there be – he had concluded, as we might, that doing is action. That this conclusion is simplistic is shown in the next verse:

कर्मणो ह्यपि बोद्धव्यं बोद्धव्यं च विकर्मण: ।
अकर्मणश्च बोद्धव्यं गहना कर्मणो गति: ॥ ४-१७ ॥

Karmaṇo hyapi boddhavyaṁ boddhavyaṁ ca vikarmaṇaḥ
Akarmaṇaśca boddhavyaṁ gahanā karmaṇo gatiḥ (IV:17)

The true nature of (enjoined) action should be known, as the truth of prohibited action and inaction is difficult (to know).

The true nature of action and actionlessness should be understood, because it is not as obvious as Arjuna thinks. The nature of action is change, motion. In this context inaction may be understood as absence of activity. Arjuna wants to renounce all actions to achieve actionlessness, so that he could become free from action, and thus become full. Can actionlessness be achieved by renouncing action? Can one become free from action by renouncing action?

An action is performed in order to achieve a desired end. You think that you are not happy, and so you desire to gain happiness by achieving something. The desire to be happy becomes a desire for a specific end, which you try to achieve by action. Thus when desire is the *basis* of action, how can desires disappear merely by giving up action? Even if one takes to *sannyāsa,* the life of a renouncer, action is given up but the desire persists. The only change is that now there is no way of fulfilling the desires, because one has renounced action. This is a situation ideal for frustration. If Arjuna pursued this path he would be only a frustrated person; merely taking *sannyāsa* cannot help anyone gain knowledge. In Chapter 3 the Lord had said:

न कर्मणामनारम्भान्नैष्कर्म्यं पुरुषोऽश्नुते ।
न च सन्न्यसनादेव सिद्धिं समधिगच्छति ॥ ३-४ ॥

Na karmaṇāmanārambhānnaiṣkarmyaṁ puruṣo'śnute
Na ca sannyasanādeva siddhiṁ samadhigacchati (III: 4)

One does not achieve actionlessness by non-performance of action; nor does one gain what is to be gained (actionlessness), by mere renunciation of action.

From this verse it is clear that *naiṣkarmya*, actionlessness, is not a mere absence of activity. Actionlessness is viewed from an entirely different standpoint, one that challenges your fundamental conclusions about yourself.

You Are Actionless Awareness

The very fact that you want to renounce action shows that you take yourself to be a *kartā*—a doer, an actor. But are you really an actor? No one can renounce what one does not have. In the vision of the Gita, you are not an actor. If you are not an actor, how can you give up action?

We have concluded that we act, we perceive, we think; but upon analysis these conclusions are seen to be false. Let us consider a single act, speaking. If asked, "Who are you?", you may answer, "I am the speaker." We could ask next, "Isn't the voice box the speaker? You cannot speak without it." You may then answer that you are the voice box as well; and that you are also the sound that is produced and also the thought behind the intelligible sound. Were you there before the thought arose in your mind? You were. Then who are you? You might say that you are the mind. But in a fainting fit the mind does not think nor does it cognise, and still you know you were there, even when you had fainted.

Finally you have to admit that you are really not the speaker, nor the listener, nor the thinker, but a conscious being capable of speaking, listening, and thinking. Does that conscious being act? It does not. You are that being, that Awareness, in whose presence actions, perceptions, and thoughts take place. When you say, "I perform action," it is not Awareness that performs any action. It is the eyes which see, the thoughts which move in the mind, all in Awareness, in consciousness.

Action is of the nature of movement. All actions stand in I, Awareness, the consciousness that is aware of time and space. The planets, the air, the people, all move only in Awareness. Space itself is in Awareness, so Awareness must be all-pervasive. Where can it move? Awareness, I, is motionless. It is that which is always present, in which even time continuously moves. Awareness is thus timeless. You are that Awareness in which all things exist, but which itself is free from time and space. Therefore,

कर्मण्यकर्म यः पश्येदकर्मणि च कर्म यः ।
स बुद्धिमान्मनुष्येषु स युक्तः कृत्स्नकर्मकृत् ॥ ४–१८ ॥

Karmaṇyakarma yaḥ paśyedakarmaṇi ca karma yaḥ
Sa buddhimānmanuṣyeṣu sa yuktaḥ kṛtsnakarmakṛt

(IV:18)

The one who sees the actionless in action, and action in inaction is wise among men; he is a *yogī*, one who has achieved all that is to be achieved.

Action takes place in Awareness, which is actionless. This is one's real nature. One who appreciates oneself as actionless does not take oneself to be an actor, in spite of acting. I recognise that the mind, sense organs, and limbs perform their respective tasks, and I am the one Awareness blessing them all. In my presence all activities take place, but I do not perform any action. Only one who knows oneself in this manner is called liberated, not one who has merely given up action.

An Illustration of Actionlessness

A man once rode in his chauffeur-driven car to visit a friend in a neighbouring town. Upon arriving, he said to his friend, "While coming here today, I did sixty miles per hour." His friend did not wonder at this, though he knew that his obese friend could not even walk sixty steps. He understood that he had come in a car, and that it is the car which did the moving, while his friend sat relaxed in the back seat. When the man said that he did sixty miles per hour it was only with reference to the car in which he was riding; as for himself, he did nothing.

Similarly, Awareness, I, never performs any action. This I is like that man seated in the car; the car moves and the man appears to move also. So too, when the body acts, it looks as though this I acts; when it is the body that talks and walks, people think that I acts. From its own standpoint the I is actionless. The one who knows and lives this is always relaxed, and is *kṛtsnakarmakṛt,* one who has achieved everything that is to be achieved — freedom from all limitations.

Arjuna finds it difficult to understand this teaching because of the impurities of his mind, his likes and dislikes. They, not Duryodhana, are his real enemies. With this in mind, the Lord exhorts him, "If you are unable to understand your nature to be actionlessness, perform action with the right attitude so that your mind becomes pure, capable of understanding what I have taught. Purification of the mind is achieved by *karma yoga*. Therefore, Arjuna, arise and perform your duty."

9
Renunciation

Lord Kṛṣna's teaching has shown that Arjuna's plan to attain happiness by renouncing action is based on a lack of understanding. Arjuna's problems are not caused by action and its results, but by his own likes and dislikes. They will continue to haunt him whether he acts or not. In fact, only by performing action with the attitude of *karma yoga* can he remove his likes and dislikes, the source of his problems.

Having first taught Arjuna the purpose of *karma yoga* Lord Kṛṣṇa also shows him the true meaning of renunciation. Giving up action is not renunciation, for giving up presupposes that one is actually controlling an action. This notion is an error. One must see what it is that performs action. You are aware of all your mental and physical activities, and of the faculties that perform these; therefore, you are none of them. You are pure Awareness, *caitanya*, in whose presence all these function. You conclude that you are an actor and then resolve to renounce action while there is no action in you in the first place. Awareness is actionless.

A person who knows the Self to be actionless is ever relaxed, even when engaged in activities. A wise person renounces the *notion* that he or she is the actor, having discovered the actionless nature of the Self. This is the true meaning of renunciation.

सर्वकर्माणि मनसा सन्न्यस्यास्ते सुखं वशी ।
नवद्वारे पुरे देही नैव कुर्वन्न कारयन् ।। ५-१३ ।।

Sarvakarmāṇi manasā sannyasyāste sukhaṁ vaśī
Navadvāre pure dehī naiva kurvanna kārayan (V:13)

Renouncing all action by knowledge, he sits happily in this nine-gated city (this physical body), neither acting nor causing anyone to act.

I, Awareness, is present everywhere all the time; in my presence the eyes, the mind and the limbs function; in me the thoughts move, the planets move; in me is the whole time-space framework. Even the notion of non-existence is in the all-pervasive Awareness. Being all-pervasive, Awareness cannot move; it performs no action. Thus, I, Awareness, is actionless. To know this is to renounce action. One who has this knowledge is not afraid of action; he or she is poised and at peace.

At this stage a doubt may arise. If one has to discover actionlessness by knowledge, what is the purpose of renouncing action? Why should there be an order of *sannyāsa,* as it is described in the Śruti and also in the Gita? What is the place of this special lifestyle if renunciation of action is only to be achieved by knowledge, rather than by actually giving up action? Arjuna might well have asked these questions, for his understanding is this: there are two styles of living, each of which can help one to achieve *śreyas.* One is the life of renunciation and the other the life of activity. There can be release in both, and there can be bondage in both, depending upon one's attitude. Arjuna thinks that one has a choice between action and renunciation. Because of his strong desire to avoid the war he faces, Arjuna naturally thinks that if one has a choice between these two lifestyles, one would eagerly choose the life of a *sannyāsī*, one exempt from duty to the society. To understand the error in Arjuna's thinking, one must see *sannyāsa* in the context of the Hindu society.

Duty, Renunciation and Sannyāsa

The Hindu society is duty-based. A wife has a duty to help her husband, and the husband in turn has a duty to make her happy. If each performs his or her duty, the rights of the other are assured, and there is no conflict between them. If, on the other hand, one or the other ignores the duty and only clamours for his or her rights, there is bound to be conflict.

Human beings are social beings; therefore they have duties to the society, to the family, to the country, to humanity, even to the elements of nature. A king is the trustee of the kingdom; it is his duty to govern the citizens fairly. A citizen has a duty to defend the country and support the king. A parent has a duty to bring out the best in the child. Each of us has a duty to care for the earth, air, and water from which we take our sustenance. In the third chapter of the Gita, Lord Kṛṣṇa says that one who only takes from others and does not fulfil his duties is a thief. If you benefit from the society but do not invest in it, you are a thief. We live by mutually helping one another and so we have definite duties towards one another. Discharging these duties gladly is *karma yoga.*

Since society is duty-based, a person should perform his or her duty until he or she is motivated by the desire for *mokṣa,* liberation. After leading a life of *karma yoga* for many years, your attitude will change. You will no longer be swayed by likes and dislikes, but will be objective instead and see clearly that the only goal in life is liberation. Then the state of the mind will be, "I don't want anything in this life or in the life hereafter; I don't long for security or pleasures. I am not interested in these; I do not seek them."

When you have reached this level of understanding, a choice is given to you. You may continue to perform actions with a dutiful attitude while you puruse Self-knowledge by studying with a teacher, or you may become a *sannyāsī,* a renouncer, leading a life entirely dedicated to study and contemplation.

A *sannyāsī* does not participate in the society; he or she has no obligation to the family or the community and is not governed by anyone. A *sannyāsī* 's only obligation is to engage in study and reflection, to acknowledge the fact revealed by the Śruti that the Self is limitless. Society supports such a person and treats him or her with reverence. No *sādhu* (mendicant monk) starves to death, but at the same time no one becomes a *sādhu* with the expectation that the society will support him or her. Any society will take care of a person who wants to lead the life of a monk, a contemplative life dedicated to the pursuit of knowledge.

Praise of Knowledge and Arjuna's Doubt

Arjuna's confusion about which lifestyle to choose persists because the Lord repeatedly tells him to perform action and at the same time he repeatedly praises knowledge as the direct means of liberation.

अपि चेदसि पापेभ्यः सर्वेभ्यः पापकृत्तमः ।
सर्वं ज्ञानप्लवेनैव वृजिनं सन्तरिष्यसि ॥ ४-३६ ॥

Api cedasi pāpebhyassarvebhyaḥ pāpakṛttamaḥ
Sarvaṁ jñānaplavenaiva vṛjinaṁ santariṣyasi (IV:36)

Even if you are the most sinful among all sinners, you will still surely cross this ocean of sin by the raft of knowledge.

Condemning oneself as a sinner is the result of ignorance. Sins, wrong actions, belong to the actor, not to the Actionless. If you discover yourself to be Actionless, where is your sin? By this knowledge you will transcend all sorrow; if you know what you are, the problem is solved. Just as a dreamer who has committed multiple murders in dream is innocent upon waking, so too you are free from all sins when you wake up to the knowledge that you are actionless Awareness.

In the fourth chapter of the Gita Lord Kṛṣṇa praises the knowledge that releases one from all sorrow. *Na hi jñānena sadṛsaṁ pavitramiha vidyate:* There is nothing as purifying as knowledge; *jñānāgniḥ sarvakarmāṇi bhasmasātkurute:* The fire of knowledge consumes every sin. Arjuna might well have expressed his confusion thus: "You praise knowledge again and again. While fighting, what knowledge will I get except that of the wailing of widows? Please tell me why I should fight. Why should I not take up the life of a *sannyāsī?*
Again in the fifth chapter we find Arjuna's question:

सन्न्यासं कर्मणां कृष्ण पुनर्योगं च शंससि ।
यच्छ्रेय एतयोरेकं तन्मे ब्रूहि सुनिश्चितम् ॥ ५-१ ॥

Sannyāsaṁ karmanāṁ kṛṣṇa punaryogāṁ ca 'samsasi
Yacchāreya etayorekaṁ tanme brūhi suniścitaṁ (V:1)

You praise renunciation of all action. O Kṛṣṇa, and again its performance. Tell me definitely which of the two is better.

Arjuna has not become wiser by the teaching of the third and the fourth chapters. At the start of the fifth chapter his question is the same : "Why praise the life of renunciation on the one hand and ask me to perform action on the other? Both cannot lead to the same goal. Is it not that action binds, while renunciation releases? Tell me clearly what is proper for me. I am ready to follow to the letter whatever you say."

Renunciation and Action : Their Roles

Arjuna's confusion is understandable, but the Lord cannot tell him which of these lifestyles is better because they are not alternatives, just as one cannot answer the question, "Shall I go to college or get the degree?" Going to college is the means and the degree is the end — one is not better than the other. Similarly, *karma yoga* is a necessary preparation for the life of a renouncer, a life dedicated to the pursuit of knowledge. Since Lord Kṛṣṇa cannot give Arjuna any clear-cut choice, his reply only seems to prolong the confusion.

सन्न्यासः कर्मयोगश्च निःश्रेयसकरावुभौ ।
तयोस्तु कर्मसन्न्यासात्कर्मयोगो विशिष्यते ॥ ५-२ ॥

Sannyāsaḥ karmayogaśca niśśreyakarāvubhau
Tayostu karmasannyāsātkarmayogo viśiṣyate (V: 2)

Both *sannyāsa* and *karma yoga* lead to liberation. Of these two, however, *karma yoga* is better than the renunciation of action.

By this answer Lord Kṛṣṇa is not recommending *karma yoga* in preference to *sannyāsa*. He tries to make Arjuna see that there is no choice between these two: rather, one adopts the life for which one is suited. What is achieved by *sannyāsa* can be achieved equally well by a life of action if one's attitude is right. That is why Lord Kṛṣṇa says that both *sannyāsa* and *karma* help one discover liberation. But *sannyāsa* is very difficult if one does not possess a contemplative mind. *Karma yoga* gives one a contemplative mind, capable of discovering the fact that true *sannyāsa* is renunciation of action by the knowledge that the I is actionless.

Lord Kṛṣṇa repeats the need for *karma yoga* in a later verse:

सन्न्यासस्तु महाबाहो दुःखमाप्तुमयोगतः ॥ ५-६ ॥

Sannyāsastu mahābāho duḥkhamāptumayogataḥ (V: 6)

O mighty-armed one, without *karma yoga, sannyāsa* is very difficult to achieve.

Lord Kṛṣṇa means that the one who takes to *sannyāsa* before developing a contemplative mind through the practice of *karma yoga,* will only denigrate the very order of *sannyāsa,* for one who takes *sannyāsa* even when one is unprepared is only a beggar, a nuisance to the society as well as to oneself. Arjuna has not developed a contemplative mind. He has just begun to analyse the problem of limitation and sorrow and is seeking a solution. His likes and dislikes are still very much part of him and cannot be given up at will. He cannot take to *sannyāsa* so easily.

Nyāsa and Sannyāsa

At heart, everyone is interested in *sannyāsa* – every one of us keeps only a minimum of possessions, things without which we feel we would be unhappy. The moment we discover that we do not need an object, we give it up readily. Thus our heart lies only in renunciation.

What everyone needs most is freedom; we do not wish to depend on anyone or anything for our happiness. This dependence on things and beings for one's happiness is called *saṁsāra.* Mere possession of things does not cause the bondage of *saṁsāra,* but if there is a thing whose absence makes you unhappy, you are bound. If you give up a thing deliberately, yet continue to feel that your happiness depends upon it you will suffer; you are still a *saṁsāri,* not a *sannyāsī.*

The meaning of any Sanskrit word is revealed by the root from which it is derived. The word *sannyāsa* is formed by adding prefix *saṁ* to the word *nyāsa* which is derived from the root *as* with the prefix *ni.. Nyāsa* means renunciation. The prefix *saṁ* enhances the meaning of the word; thus, *sannyāsa* means total renunciation.

What is total renunciation? In what way is *sannyāsa* different from *nyāsa?* If one gives up something out of grief or pride, for example, the renunciation is only *nyāsa.* When, however, one gives up something and does not have any sense of loss or relief, one enjoys *sannyāsa*.

Who is not familiar with *nyāsa?* If a young boy's father tells him that he is now too old to play marbles and that he should give it up and play cricket instead, the boy may give up playing marbles. He may even give away his marble collection to his younger brother. But he is a marble-*nyāsi,* not *sannyāsī*, because he has still a taste for the game; on seeing other boys playing marbles, he stops to watch. The Lord had said earlier:

विषया विनिवर्तन्ते निराहारस्य देहिनः । रसवर्जम्........ ॥ २–५९ ॥

Viṣayā vinivartante nirāhārasya dehinaḥ
Rasavarjaṁ... (II : 59)

Sense objects fall away from one who abstains, but the taste (for them) remains.

The next day, the boy will avoid going to the place where other boys are playing marbles, because he knows that watching them will only tempt him to play. Such an attitude is not *sannyāsa,* but *nyāsa,* for the boy has a sense of loss for what he has given up.

However, when the boy grows up to become a grandfather and his grandson asks him to play marbles with him, he has no hesitation in doing that. Why? The sight of marbles does not arouse any longing in him now, and their absence also does not cause regret. The marbles are no longer important to him. Now he is not a *nyāsi,* but a *sannyāsī* — with regard to marbles.

ज्ञेयः स नित्यसन्न्यासी यो न द्वेष्टि न काङ्क्षति ।
निर्द्वन्द्वो हि महाबाहो सुखं बन्धात्प्रमुच्यते ॥ ५–३ ॥

Jñeyassa nityasannyāsyī yo na dveṣṭi na kāṅksṣati
Nirdvandvo hi mahābāho sukhaṁ bandhāt pramucyate
(V:3)

Know him to be always a *sannyāsī* who neither hates nor longs for anything. Indeed, O mighty-armed one, one who is free from the pairs of opposites (joy and sorrow, pleasure and pain, and so on) is easily liberated from bondage.

Having outgrown the fascination for childhood games, you are a marble-*sannyāsī*. If the entire world holds for you no more attraction than those marbles, if your heart has found that fullness and maturity, you are truly a *sannyāsī*.

It is now clear that shunning action cannot make you a *sannyāsī*. You cannot choose *sannyāsa;* it has to be discovered. It is the recognition of yourself as a full and free being who is not dependent upon anything for happiness that makes you a *sannyāsī*. Just as you cannot ask someone to love you or order a flower to bloom, so too, you cannot order *sannyāsa*. You have to wait for it to happen, while performing actions with the right attitude. This world has everything you need to bloom into a flower of maturity. A composed mind, the result of a life of *karma yoga*, will find *sannyāsa* naturally.

नैव किञ्चित्करोमीति युक्तो मन्येत तत्त्ववित् ।
पश्यञ्शृण्वन्स्पृशञ्जिघ्रन्नश्नन्गच्छन्स्वपञ्श्वसन् ॥ ५-८ ॥

प्रलपन्विसृजन्गृह्णन्नुन्मिषन्निमिषन्नपि ।
इन्द्रियाणीन्द्रियार्थेषु वर्तन्त इति धारयन् ॥ ५-९ ॥

Naiva kiñcitkaromīti yukto manyeta tattvavit
Paśyañśṛṇvanspṛśañjighrannaśnangacchansvapañśvasan (V:8)

Pralapanvisṛjangṛhṇannunmiṣannimiṣannapi
Indriyāṇīndriyārtheṣu vartanta iti dhārayan (V:9)

One who knows the truth knows, "I never perform action", even while performing all actions, such as seeing, hearing, touching, smelling, eating, walking, sleeping, breathing, speaking, letting go, grasping, and opening and closing the eyes — knowing that it is the sense organs that move among the sense objects.

One who knows the Self that is actionless knows that I, Awareness, blesses the mind that directs the sense organs and organs of action to act. I, Awareness, never performs any action. This person is a *sannyāsī*. To gain this knowledge, one must discover a contemplative mind, and for that *karma* is necessary. So get ready for action, O Arjuna, and act with the right attitude.

10
Meditation

Sannyāsa, renunciation, is neither a mental nor a physical act; it requires an abiding mind, but it is not a psychological state. Renunciation is the knowledge that the real meaning of I is actionlesness; the Self is free from any action — physical, perceptual or mental. One who knows that the Self performs no action, even when one is physically engaged in action is a renouncer, a *sannyāsī.*

There is, however, a style of living called *sannyāsa,* a life of renunciation, which is contemplative rather than active. When the mind has become contemplative there is no desire for action and one can engage in *ātma-vicāra,* inquiry into the nature of the Self. This mind will discover freedom. If a person merely copies this lifestyle, it will not necessarily change the quality of the mind (although such a change is possible if, for example, one gives up bad company and turns to people who are interested in *vicāra*), but if one changes the quality of one's mind, one's lifestyle will definitely change. Therefore, in teaching Arjuna, who longs for *sannyāsa,* the Lord emphasises the development of a contemplative mind, a mind free from likes and dislikes, a mind that is naturally more abiding than reactive, a mind that is able to see things clearly, a mind that observes without judging, a mind that is naturally smiling, not subject to easy excitement. Such a mind is contemplative and capable of learning.

You cannot *decide* to be contemplative, just as you cannot decide to be loving. You can decide not to talk or not to eat or to do *yogāsanas,* but you cannot decide that you will love someone from today. A person who is not contemplative cannot decide to be contemplative. So too, a person who is contemplative cannot be otherwise, regardless of his or her location or activities. If one does not have a mind suitable for contemplation, *karma yoga* is necessary; action performed with the proper attitude is the means of gaining a contemplative mind. Therefore there is no choice between a life of action and a life of contemplation; action is the means by which one gains a mind suited to a life of inquiry and contemplation, so that Self-knowledge, which is true renunciation, can be gained. Arjuna asked the Lord to tell him which of these two — action or renunciation — is better, but Lord Kṛṣṇa does not name one, for there is no choice between the means and the end. One must employ the means to gain the end. In the sixth chapter, the Lord says:

आरुरुक्षोर्मुनेर्योगं कर्म कारणमुच्यते ॥
योगारूढस्य तस्यैव शमः कारणमुच्यते ॥ ६–३ ॥

Ārurukṣormuneryogam karma kāraṇamucyate
Yogārūḍhasya tasyaiva śamaḥ kāraṇamucyate (VI: 3)

Karma yoga is said to be the means for a discriminating person who wants to master contemplation; renunciation is said to be the means for one who has already mastered contemplation.

Experience Is Not Knowledge

Renunciation is recognising your own nature, full and complete, never changing. The ignorance and error that cause you to be estranged from this truth can be removed only by knowledge gained through the teaching of Vedanta. You may have various experiences of joy and fullness, but experience will not give you the knowledge that you are *sat-cit-ānanda*. You will keep trying to create circumstances that lead you to more such experiences. We all experience happiness, but we want lasting happiness, continuous happiness. Each of us seems to have a standard by which we judge our prevailing frame of mind. We say that we want a more profound experience because we have known that most profound experience, that deepest joy. When you discover something especially beautiful, your mind clears for a moment and you capture a moment of perfect joy. That experience will remain in your mind as a standard by which all other experiences will be judged, and you will continue to search for the means to have that happiness for ever. What is the source of that happiness?

Imagine that a great devotee goes on foot from the

southern tip of India to Badrīnāth, far in the north. He reaches the temple in Badrīnāth, totally exhausted, having had to overcome many seemingly insurmountable difficulties on the way, but he is full of joy at having at last reached the temple. He goes inside and stands in front of the idol, and in the ecstasy of seeing the Lord of his heart, he closes his eyes. Why should he make the difficult journey all the way from the southern tip of India only to close his eyes when he is finally standing in front of the Lord whom he has come so far to see? He closes his eyes not because they are tired, not because he has already seen enough; his eyes close because he has gained what he desired most. He had been seeking the Lord. When the seeker finally reaches the sought there is a moment of fulfilment in which the seeker and the sought are fused. The eyes have achieved their purpose, and they close. In this moment of fulfilment, the pilgrim does not see God as a deity, nor himself as a devotee. God and the devotee resolve into each other; duality disappears.

In a moment of profound happiness, the duality of the knower and the known, the seer and the seen disappears. There is only one flame of *advaita*, non-duality, that has no limitation in time or space. In that moment of fullness, the desire to be limitless is fulfilled; there is nothing other than you. The fullness that obtains in that experience is not due to any object or situation; it is yourself, free of the taxing, demanding, desiring and willing mind. Unfortunately, you do not recognize that fullness is your very nature. Experience does not give you knowledge; it only gives you a height at which you want to abide, and you cannot settle for anything less. To know that fullness is yourself, you require knowledge, and for gaining that knowledge teaching is necessary.

What Is Knowledge?

The teacher cites such moments in which the joy of non-duality is experienced, and tells the student, "*Tattvamasi*: That (limitlessness) thou art." You are *nityāsannyāsta*, action-less. You are *cit*, self-effulgent Awareness.

It is in the light of the sun or moon or any other sources of light that objects are revealed to your eyes. These source of light shine, that is, they appear effulgent, because your eyes are bright. If your eyes had no light, the sun would not shine — it does not shine for a blind man. Your eyes shine because your mind shines; the eyes see, the ears hear, the nose smells, the tongue tastes, because an effulgent mind is behind these sense organs. The mind shines because you shine; you light up the mind, you are the seer of the mind. All these — the mind, the sense organs, all sources of light — shine because you shine and you shine because you cannot but shine; you are self-effulgent Awareness, requiring no other source of light.

During Hindu rituals, a piece of burning camphor is held up to the altar. The *mantra*[1] that is chanted while waving this camphor light before the deity, describes the effulgent nature of the Self:

न तत्र सूर्यो भाति न चन्द्रतारकं
नेमा विद्युतो भान्ति कुतोऽयमग्निः ।
तमेव भान्तमनुभाति सर्वं
तस्य भासा सर्वमिदं विभाति ॥
—कठोपनिषद् २-२-१५

Na tatra sūryo bhāti na candra tārakaṁ
nemā vidyuto bhānti kutoyamagniḥ
Tameva bhāntamanubhāti sarvam
tasya bhāsā sarvamidaṁ vibhāti
(Kaṭhopaniṣad II:2:15)

There (in Awareness, the Self) the sun shines not, nor does the moon nor the stars. Even lightning does not shine there; what to talk of this fire (the light of camphor)? That (Self) shining, all else shines because of it. The effulgence of that (Self) illumines all the universe.

Through this *mantra* you appreciate that you are the Awareness by which all the world is known. A person who appreciates this fact, revealed by the teaching, is wise. That person knows that he or she does not act; blessed by Awareness, the mind acts, the sense organs do their job.

1. A hymn or text especially from the Veda, chanted as a prayer.

When one appreciates that one is actionless one is truly a *sannyāsī*, a renouncer. In order to appreciate this, you need an abiding mind, and *karma yoga* is the means of gaining that mind. Thus Lord Kṛṣṇa tells Arjuna that action is necessary for a person desirous of pursuing a contemplative life.

Self-Condemnation Is a Problem

By performing action with the right attitude, you will gain a contemplative mind. With every result received as *prasāda,* the Lord's blessing, your mind becomes purer; likes and dislikes are lessened and your mind becomes free of reactions. Eventually you will find that your mind is naturally contemplative. Although this development of the mind takes time, there is no reason for despair or frustration; never look down upon yourself or conclude that you are not fit for Self-knowledge. Self-condemnation will not help you. If others condemn you, do not accept their judgment. It is common for a person to be criticised by others even in childhood. The attempt to make you feel that you are inadequate continues throughout your life, at home, at school and in society. You are led to conclude that you are useless. Even a boastful person feels that he or she is useless, and goes about boasting to cover up the feeling of inadequacy. If you refuse to abandon this negative judgement about yourself even God cannot help you. So the Lord tells Arjuna.

उद्धरेदात्मनात्मानं नात्मानमवसादयेत् ॥ ६–५ ॥

Uddharedātmanātmānaṁ nātmānamavasādayet (VI:5)

Lift yourself by yourself. Do not condemn yourself.

Thus, Lord Kṛṣṇa prepares Arjuna's mind and tells him that all he needs is himself. Clear knowledge of the Self is liberation from all limitation; to gain freedom from limitation one does not have to do anything, for one's nature is limitlessness.

The Problem of Habit

Two problems have so far been discussed — ignorance and

error. The fear you sustain on mistaking a rope for a snake is not only due to ignorance of the rope, but is also due to the error of taking it as a snake. The clear knowledge that it is only a rope will remove both the ignorance and the error. Similarly, teaching will make you see that you are limitless; the ignorance of your nature and the error of taking yourself to be limited will go. If the teaching is imparted and you are prepared, you will see the fact of your limitlessness very clearly. If your mind is not prepared, you can act with an attitude of *karma yoga,* and the teaching will begin to make sense as your mind becomes more stable.

Now there is a third problem. Even though you have seen that the snake you so feared is only a rope, the tremor in your body, the aftermath of fear, remains for some time, Similarly, in spite of seeing the meaning of the teaching clearly, when you are away from the teacher you take yourself to be a limited person. The limitations of the physical body and mind overwhelm you; you do not seem to be able to own up to what was taught and reap its rewards. This is due to the habit of taking yourself wrongly.

Suppose a beggar wins a prize in a lottery. After years of penniless, miserable existence, he suddenly has his own car, house, every comfort that money can buy; but if he sees someone distributing alms, his age-old habit will make him run to see what is being given, and even to stretch out his hand to receive his share. In his mind the beggar-turned-rich is still poor; he has not measured up to his riches. This beggarliness will not go away immediately. To realise his new status, he must meditate upon himself as a rich man; he must constantly be aware that he is rich; he must retain this awareness of being rich. When he can do this, he need not meditate any longer; he has assimilated the fact that he is not a beggar, but a rich man.

Similarly, in day-to-day life your beggarliness comes up as you scramble to pick up crumbs of happiness thrown by the hands of chance. Being conditioned like this to be a beggar of happiness, even when you come to understand that you are *sat-cit–ānanda,* the limitless fullness that you long for, you still feel that you are inadequate and dependent. You remain beggarly in spite of being rich. This is a problem of habit. It has grown entrenched over the years, and it will take time for it to die.

The Need for Meditation

To break the habit of seeing oneself as limited, the Lord advises meditation. Forgetfulness is a common thing in the life of a human being. While watching a three-dimensional movie, even though you know you are watching a movie, you duck when you see a stone being thrown. At the moment you are ducking, you are totally identified with the movie, which means you have forgotten yourself. Similarly, one forgets one's true nature when acting in the world and becomes an impulsive being. Though one is usually rational, one is a victim of one's old habits, and one acts without thinking. How can these habits be forsaken ?

Lord Kṛṣṇa tells Arjuna to be with himself. He says:

शुचौ देशे प्रतिष्ठाप्य स्थिरमासनमात्मनः ।
नात्युच्छ्रितं नातिनीचं चैलाजिनकुशोत्तरम् ॥ ६–११ ॥
समं कायशिरोग्रीवं धारयन्नचलं स्थिरः ।
सम्प्रेक्ष्य नासिकाग्रं स्वं दिशश्चानवलोकयन् ॥ ६–१३ ॥
प्रशान्तात्मा विगतभीर्ब्रह्मचारिव्रते स्थितः ।
मनः संयम्य मच्चित्तो युक्त आसीत मत्परः ॥ ६–१४ ॥

Sucau deśe pratiṣṭhāpya sthiramāsanamātmanaḥ
Nātyucchritaṁ nāṭinīcaṁ cailājinakuṣottaraṁ (VI: 11)

Samaṁ kāyaśirogrīvaṁ dhārayannacalaṁ sthiraḥ
Samprekṣya nāsikāgraṁ svaṁ diśaścānavalokayan (VI:13)

Praśāntatmā vigatabhīrbrahmacārivrate sthitaḥ
Manassamyamya maccitto yukta āsīta matparaḥ (VI:14)

Having arranged in a clean place a firm seat that is neither too high nor too low, covered with a soft cloth, an animal skin, and kuśa grass with the body, head and neck held straight, (with the limbs) unmoving and (with the mind) steady, looking (as though) at the tip of the nose, not looking around in different directions, may the one who is very peaceful, who is free from fear, who follows the vows of a *brahmacārī*, having controlled his mind (may that one) sit steadfast, being one who thinks only of Me (the Lord), and who regards Me as Supreme.

Here the proper posture, environment, and attitude of meditation are described. Let your body, including its aches and pains, be forgotten; consciously relax the body. Arrange the seat of meditation properly; otherwise, your attention will be only on your cramped leg. Sit well so that the head, neck, and back are in a straight line, with legs folded and eyes closed, with your gaze as though directed to the tip of your nose. Having seated yourself in this posture, do not be concerned about the world. You may have appointments to keep, but you can think of them later; this is an appointment with yourself. Call a truce with the world for the time being. The sense organs are withdrawn; do not react to sounds that occur around you.

You are withdrawn, your body is relaxed. Objectify the body. See it as a stone statue. This process relaxes the body; you may not be able to visualise the exact position of your hands. Then,

तत्रैकाग्रं मनः कृत्वा यतचित्तेन्द्रियक्रियः ।
उपविश्यासने युञ्ज्याद्योगमात्मविशुद्धये ॥ ६–१२ ॥

Tatraikāgram manaḥ kṛtvā yatacittendriyakriyaḥ
Upaviśyāsane yuñjyādyogamātmaviśuddhaye (VI:12)

Seated there, having made the mind single-pointed, one who has control of the mind and senses should practise *yoga* (contemplation) to attain purity of mind.

Let the mind abide in the truth that you have discovered. You know that you are all joy, fullness, Awareness, freedom, actionlessness, motionlessness, all peace, all silence. That motionless, formless, shapeless, silence you are. Let your mind be aware of this fact. Appreciate that you are Awareness, silence — shapeless, formless silence.

शनैः शनैरुपरमेद्बुद्ध्या धृतिगृहीतया ।
आत्मसंस्थं मनः कृत्वा न किञ्चिदपि चिन्तयेत् ॥ ६–२५ ॥

Śanaiśśanairuparamedbuddhyā dhṛtigṛhītayā
Ātmasaṁsthaṁ manaḥ kṛtvā na kiñcidapi cintayet

(VI:25)

May one resolve the mind gradually by (use of) the intellect that is endowed with discrimination. Having caused the mind to abide in the Self, may one think of nothing else.

There is no need for you to think. You have thought enough for the time being. Simply appreciate yourself as formless, shapeless Awareness that is all silence. Immediately there is a release. When you think of silence, you cannot but be silence. This is the meditation that the Lord teaches Arjuna.

11

Who Is God ?

The word "I" is more abused than rightly used, for virtually everyone, because of ignorance, has erroneous notions about him. Taking a thing wrongly is error; taking it rightly, knowledge. Any conclusion that may be contradicted later is not knowledge, but an error, a notion, Knowledge, *jñāna,* is that which is not subject to negation or correction upon further inquiry; it is final, your so-called knowledge of yourself is constantly fluctuating — you are happy, you are afraid, you are free from fear; you are a success, you are a failure. Therefore, it is not really knowledge. One must be taught who one really is, as Arjuna is taught in the second chapter of the Gita. The notion of the limited "I" must be replaced by the knowledge of the limitless Self.

The Forms of Limitation

Limitation is threefold. Let us consider an object, for example, a rose. It has a form, occupying space, and thus it is spatially limited – it cannot be in two places at one time. This is called *deśa pariccheda,* limitation in regard to space. The flower also is limited in time. There was a time when it did not exist, and a time will come when it will cease to exist. Limitation in regard to time is called *kāla pariccheda.* Thirdly, the rose has qualities that make it a rose, distinct from all other objects. The rose has only rose-ness; it does not have any other attribute. This limitation is called *vastu pariccheda*, limitation in regard to qualities.

Every object in creation, including your physical body, suffers from these three forms of limitation. "I am here" means I am limited in space; "I was born" indicates limitation in time. "I wish I could swim like a fish or fly like a bird" expresses limitation in regard to qualities.

Your body, your thoughts, your knowledge, your sense

organs — all are limited. If you are this *kārya-karaṇa saṅghāta,* this body-mind complex, you are surely a limited being. But you cannot happily accept this limitation. You want to be free. Lord Kṛṣṇa explains to Arjuna that if freedom is possible, it cannot be different from oneself, as one already is. Any amount of gain cannot give one freedom, because every gain involves some loss. He tells Arjuna, "You are not the body-mind complex, for that complex is known by you as an object. You are the subject, distinct from any object of knowledge. You are *caitanya*; Awareness that has no form, and hence no limitation in space or time. The time-space limitation belongs to *kārya-karaṇa-saṅghāta,* not to the Self. Appreciate your nature as it has been unfolded; you are not limited — you are limitless."

Who Created the World?

The recognition that one's nature is Awareness brings up a question. Everything, even time and space, is in Awareness. If I am Awareness, the entire creation is in me. But who created this world? I certainly have not done so. Who created the sun and the stars? I certainly have not done so. Who made the clouds? Who formulated the laws by which all this functions. Who set the cycle of the tides and the seasons? Who provided for the needs of every creature? The world is a furnished house meant to be enjoyed by all; its kitchen serves food to every creature, be it a bee, a bird, or a man. All beings are equipped for survival; human beings come with nostrils to draw oxygen from air, a fish with gills to draw it from water. I find that nothing here is redundant. Everything is well-designed, including the human machine which is capable of lasting a hundred years. Who authored this intelligent, meaningful creation?

This desire to know the cause of something is natural to humankind. If I say, "There is a fire," you will ask for the evidence. I answer, "I see smoke, therefore there is a fire." For any inference or presumption the human intellect demands that there be a *hetu,* a cause. Without this "cause-hunting" behaviour, a human being would be like an animal, led only by the senses; there would be no inference, no presumption, no final knowledge.

The Cause of the Objective Creation

An objective creation is one that is available for perception by all observers; the object exists, and therefore you and I and others see it. This is in contrast to a subjective creation, a creation that is only perceived by its author. In a dream you see a mountain. The mountain is not an objective creation; no one but you can see it. You see it in your mind and therefore it exists.

How can one account for this objective creation? Who authored this world? For any creation there must be a creator who knows exactly what he or she is going to create and has in mind the purpose and the means of creating it. That person is called *nimitta kāraṇa*, the efficient cause, an intelligent being who has the knowledge and skill to create something particular. A potter knows what a pot is and how to make it. He knows what to use as material, how to shape it, what tools are needed — in short, the potter is one who has the knowledge and skill to make pots. A bird has the knowledge and skill to make a nest, a bee to make a honeycomb. For this world, there must be a creator who has both the knowledge of the entire creation and the power to create it.

Belief or Knowledge

If I hold a watch before you and ask you, "Do you believe that there is a maker of this watch?" your reply has to be, "Yes". You did not see anyone make the watch, but you still say that the watchmaker exists. Your conclusion is based on the same type of cause-hunting that makes it unnecessary to question and verify the existence of your great-great-grandfather though you have never seen even a picture of him; the fact that you are here is the proof that he was here before you. You are an effect that must have a cause. Though you don't know the maker of the watch, you know that there must be a maker, for any effect presupposes a cause.

Let us analyse what belief is. A belief is a judgement prior to gaining knowledge and is subject to verification by inquiry. Suppose you say, "Devadatta is a good man," even though you have never met him. You really don't know that Devadatta is good, but only believe so because someone said to you that he is good. There is every possibility that this belief can be belied. If you meet Devadatta and he does or does not turn out to be good, what you then have is not belief any longer, but knowledge about Devadatta.

Belief is not based on knowledge, and so it can always be shaken. Belief that cannot be shaken is not belief; it is knowledge. Even if a million people say that fire is cold, you will not accept it, because the fact that fire is hot is knowledge which cannot be shaken by anyone. Now remember the watch and the watchmaker. If I say that I believe in the existence of the watchmaker, his or her existence is subject to negation. Is there any possibility that the watch can be without a creator? No. Therefore, what you have is knowledge of the existence of a watchmaker, not belief.

Similarly, it is not right to say that you *believe* in God, the creator of this world. You see the creation which is intelligent and purposeful. Therefore, you don't simply believe — you *know* that there must be a creator for it. That creator should be omniscient and omnipotent, for as the potter must have the knowledge of the pot and the skill to make it, the creator of all must have all knowledge and all skill. You don't find such a being here on earth, so you imagine that He or She resides in a place, say heaven, unknown to you. You say that God in heaven created this world.

This simplistic statement will not satisfy your intellect for long. The problem now is, who created the heaven, where did God sit when He created this world? And if God created that heaven, where was God seated before the creation of heaven? This endless chain of questions arises because we fail to recognise another equally important cause of creation.

The Material Cause

For anything that is created, not only is there a creator, the intelligent cause, who has the intelligence to make it, but also there is the material with which to create. Without clay a potter cannot make pots. The material of which a thing is made is called *upādāna kāraṇa,* the material cause. The creator of the world must have needed material to create it. If that material was different from God, one could ask, who made the material? If the answer is that someone else made it, it can be argued that this someone must be considered the real creator of the world, and the question remains: from where did this new God get the material to make the world? If He made it with some other material, from where did that material come? To avoid landing in the logical absurdity of infinite regress, we must say that God Himself is the material cause of creation. God finds the material in Himself, and from it creates the world. In Muṇḍakopaniṣad, it is said,

यथोर्णनाभिः सृजते गृह्णते च...
–मुण्डकोपनिषद् १–१–७

Yathorṇaṇābhissṛjate gṛhṇate ca...
(Muṇḍakopaniṣad I:1:7)

Just as a spider spreads out and draws in (the thread that it spins)...

The spider is both *upādāna kāraṇa* and *nimitta kāraṇa,* the material of the web and the one who weaves it. Similarly, when you dream, you are the author of the dream creation, and you are also the material of it. The ocean, the mountain, the sun and moon that are so vivid in your dream are created by you out of yourself. You are both *upādāna kāraṇa* and *nimitta kāraṇa* of the dream.

This world is authored by someone who must be both its efficient and material cause. If God is the material cause, he does not stand apart from the creation. When you pick up a pot, you also pick up the material of the pot, clay; when you hold a gold chain, you hold gold. Wherever an object goes, its material cause accompanies it. The object is sustained by the material of which it is made; an effect is never separate from its material cause. If the Lord is the material and efficient cause of creation, what is the distance between the Lord and creation? There can be no distance. The Lord is the creation.

The Lord explains this to Arjuna, saying,

मत्तः परतरं नान्यत्किञ्चिदस्ति धनञ्जय ।
मयि सर्वमिदं प्रोतं सूत्रे मणिगणा इव ॥ ७–७ ॥

प्रभवः प्रलयः स्थानं निधानं बीजमव्ययम् ॥ ९-१८ ॥

मया ततमिदं सर्वं जगदव्यक्तमूर्तिना ।
मत्स्थानि सर्वभूतानि न चाहं तेष्ववस्थितः ॥ ९-४ ॥

Mattaḥ prataram nānyatkiñcidasti dhanañjaya
Mayi sarvamidaṁ protaṁ sūtre maṇigaṇā iva (VII:7)

Prabhavaḥ pralayassthānaṁ nidhānaṁ bījamavyayaṁ
(IX:18)

Maya tatamidaṁ sarvaṁ jagadavyaktamūrtinā
Matsthāni sarvabhūtāni na cāhaṁ teṣvavasthitaḥ (IX:4)

There is nothing superior to (no cause other than) Me, Arjuna; all this (world) is woven in Me like beads on a string. I am (that from which) the creation (is born that in which it finds), resolution, and (that by which it finds) sustenance, the storehouse (the source of what will be enjoyed in the future), and the indestructible seed (the source of all growth). By Me, whose nature is unmanifest (not available for perception), all this world is pervaded. All beings abide in Me, but I am not in them.

What Lord Kṛṣṇa means in these verses is this : "I am the author and the material cause of creation. Space, time, stars, sun, moon, earth, trees, seeds, men, women, all are in Me. All these came from Me and will get resolved in Me. I am not separate from the creation; don't take Me as one who is seated in heaven watching you!"

The same truth is expressed in Īśāvāsya Upaniṣad:

ईशावास्यमिदं सर्वं यत्किञ्च जगत्यां जगत् ।
–ईशावास्योपनिषद् १

Īśāvasyamidaṁ sarvaṁ yatkiñca jagatyāṁ jagat
(Īśāvāsya Upaniṣad:1)

All this, whatever moves on earth, is pervaded by the Lord.

Now tell me, where should you search for Bhagavān, the Lord? You are Bhagavān.The Lord says, "I am the material of which you are made; the fire, air, water, everything in you is Myself. Therefore, remember there is nothing that is apart from Me."

How can you search for God unless you have concluded that God is away from you? A man never searches for his head. In this conclusion that you are to seek God and see God, there is the inherent error that God is different from you. To err, that is to conclude before gaining knowledge, is the habit of a non-thinking, immature mind. Before knowledge, you cannot conclude; after knowledge, conclusion is unnecessary, for knowledge is itself conclusive, not subject to interpretation or negation.

What Is the Lord's Form?

If the Lord were to appear before you in a given form, it would be an error to conclude that He has only that form. A God limited by form would be like any other limited being and would not deserve worship. The Lord is the entire creation and so all forms are His forms; therefore, one can invoke the Lord in any form. The Lord in the form of Śri. Kṛṣṇa teaches Arjuna, "There is nothing beyond Me. I am the author of creation, and in Me everything merges."

If Arjuna had asked Lord Kṛṣṇa, "What is that I that is the omniscient, all-pervasive creator?" He would have replied that "I is the Awareness because of which I am aware of My omniscient, omnipotent, and omnipresent form." If after this teaching anyone were asked," What is the I in you, the limited one?" one would say, "The I in me is the Awareness because of which I know my limited knowledge, limited power, and limited form."

There are not two limitless Awarenesses; the same Awareness is I for both you and the Lord, and everything exists and moves in that Awareness. If your reference is not placed in your body or sense organs but in the limitless Awareness, you can say, "In me the whole world exists." Each of you can say the same if you understand what has been taught here.

The Wave and the Ocean

A small wave in the ocean saw that it was rapidly

approaching the shore where its brief life would end. Seeing a huge breaker following close behind it, the little wave wailed, "Please protect me; I am so small, a mortal wave about to meet my end. Please save me from destruction."

The breaker smiled at the wave's foolishness, but answered comfortingly, "Don't be afraid. You cannot be destroyed, for you are not just a momentary wave. You are water which is the unchanging truth of this whole ocean that created you. The ocean is the Lord that has created you, me, and countless other waves. That ocean pervades us all, and in time we will resolve into it again. You are not different from that ocean; you are water, the ocean is water. If you understand this, you will see that you are not mortal; there can be no destruction for you."

As both the ocean and the wave are the same water, the Lord and you are one limitless Awareness. In you, Awareness, is the whole creation; in you is the Lord.

12
The Self is Brahman

God is Not Different from Me

Any creation has two causes: *nimitta kāraṇa*, the efficient cause, the intelligent being who has the knowledge and skill to produce the creation; and *upādāna kāraṇa*, the material cause, the material of which a thing is made. The Lord says to Arjuna, "I am indeed the One from whom the creation is born, and what is born of Me is sustained by Me and resolves in Me alone." This statement means that the Lord is not merely the efficient cause of creation, but the material cause as well, for at the end of its existence an object resolves not into its efficient cause, but into its material cause. The pot does not resolve into the potter, but only into clay. Therefore the Lord says, "There is nothing beyond Me or other than Me in creation. No object stands apart from Me, for I am the very cause of the time-space continuum and everything that exists in it."

Humankind has not really created anything. We only rearrange, making combinations of what the Lord has already created. When we discover that the Lord has provided for all our needs, we naturally want to offer our thanks, but we find that the object of our prayers is beyond our comprehension. When we do not know what God is, we use this well-known *śloka*(verse) as our prayer:

तव तत्त्वं न जानामि कीदृशोऽसि महेश्वर ।
यादृशोऽसि महादेव तादृशाय नमो नमः ॥

Tava tattvaṁ na jānāmi kīdṛśo'si maheśvara
Yādṛśo'si mahādeva tādṛśaya namo namaḥ

I don't know the truth of you, or what you are like, O Lord. Whatever and wherever you are, may this salutation reach you.

This is a very practical form of prayer indeed. Even if your understanding of the Lord's form or whereabouts is mistaken, this prayer will reach its destination.

Once you correctly appreciate that God is the material cause of creation, you will realize that you need not go anywhere to look for Him. God is space, air, fire, water, earth; whatever there is in the universe. Anything that exists in time and space — including your physical body, sense organs, and mind — anything that is created is the Lord. Kṛṣṇa says:

अहं कृत्स्नस्य जगत: प्रभव: प्रलयस्तथा ॥ ७-६ ॥

Aham kṛtsnasya jagataḥ prabhavaḥ pralayastathā

(VII:6)

I am the cause of origin of the entire world and so too of its dissolution.

Because the Lord is the material cause of creation, you may say, "I know the creation, and therefore I know the Lord;" but the Lord cannot be an object of your knowledge, for an object has to be different from you, the subject. The Lord is not different from you. If everything were different from the Lord, what would be left of the Lord would be precious little. If you imagine that you can look upon the Lord as an object, you are making yourself superior to Him. If God were an object of your thought, separate from you, you could dismiss the object, God, and continue to exist, thinking of something else. The Lord would fall in the category of something that comes and goes, depending on your thought; God is then no different from any other limited being. This situation arises out of a wrong understanding of what God is.

Who Is a Devotee?

When one invokes the Lord in prayer, one is demonstrating that one knows that God exists. If one does not appreciate, however, that the Lord and oneself are identical, one's knowledge of the Lord is incomplete. In the seventh chapter such incomplete knowledge is called *jñāna*; one who has this partial knowledge — Who knows that God is — is called an *āstika*.

Waves are born of the ocean; by the ocean they are sustained, and unto the ocean they resolve. A wave is related to the ocean as an individual is related to God. The ocean inheres every wave, yet the wave looks upon the ocean as different from itself. It thinks, "The limitless ocean created me, a limited wave." Of course, the wave's appreciation of the existence of its creator, the ocean, is a big leap in thinking as compared to that of the idiotic wave which thinks it came from heaven or that there is nothing beyond itself. Since it appreciates that the ocean is the efficient cause of its birth, this wave is an *āstika,* a devotee. It knows that the ocean *asti,* is; just as you know you had a great-great-grandfather.

Three Types of Devotees

There are three types of devotees: *ārta,* one who is stricken, *arthārthī,* one who seeks some gain, and *jijñāsu,* one who desires to know God. All have *jñāna,* the partial knowledge that the Lord exists, but they do not know that the Lord is not separate from themselves.

Ārta is a person who is stricken; when his life is in shambles, he throws up his arms and implores the Lord to help him. He feels that only the Lord can extricate him from the situation in which he has landed. He accepts the Lord's power and seeks His help.

The second type of devotee is *arthārthī,* a person who desires some gain. In this case, one knows that one has to put in an effort to get whatever one wants — one does not depend solely on God — but also appreciates the necessity of *daiva,* God. The prayer is *karma,* an action, and like any action it will produce a result. The devotee knows that God is the wielder of the laws and *karmaphaladātā,* the giver of the results of all action; so any offering invoking God's grace will be efficacious. One's prayer may be *kāyika,* in the form of physical action such as offering a flower, *vācika,* in the form of speech, singing the Lord's glories, or *mānasa,* purely mental. What is offered is immaterial. Lord Kṛṣṇa says:

पत्रं पुष्पं फलं तोयं यो मे भक्त्या प्रयच्छति ।
तदहं भक्त्युपहृतमश्नामि प्रयतात्मनः ॥ ९–२६ ॥

Patram puṣpaṁ phalaṁ toyaṁ yo me bhaktyā prayacchati
Tadahaṁ bhaktyupahṛtamaśnāmi prayatātmanaḥ (IX: 26)

Anything that is offered with devotion — be it a leaf, flower, fruit or water — that I enjoy, coming from one whose mind is pure.

Like *ārta* and *arthārthī,* the third type of devotee also does not know God very well, but he is not interested in the limited ends sought by the other two. He only wants to know the truth about himself, the Lord and the world. He is called *jijñāsu,* one who is desirous of direct knowledge. He seeks the Lord's help in gaining knowledge.

All three enjoy some *jñāna.* Each one knows that the Lord exists. One wants the Lord to help him, another wants the Lord to give him something, the third wants to gain knowledge of the Lord. Of these three, *jijñāsu* is the most fortunate, for he knows that chasing ends in life only solves small problems, that others are doing this because they have not realized that the basic problem of limitation cannot be solved by any amount of gain. *Jijñāsu* knows that freedom from limitation can only be gained by knowing oneself to be free; he wants to know God as himself.

The Fourth Type of Devotee

We have discussed three types of devotees, but Lord Kṛṣṇa mentions four types of devotees:

चतुर्विधा भजन्ते मां जनाः सुकृतिनोऽर्जुन ।
आर्तो जिज्ञासुरर्थार्थी ज्ञानी च भरतर्षभ ॥ ७-१६ ॥
उदाराः सर्व एवैते ज्ञानी त्वात्मैव मे मतम् ॥ ७-१८ ॥

Caturvidhā bhajante māṁ janāssukṛtino'rjuna
Ārto jijñāsurarthārthī jñānī ca bharatarṣabha (VII:16)

Udārāḥ sarva evaite jñānī tvātmaiva me mataṁ (VII:18)

Four kinds of people worship me, Arjuna: one who is distressed, one who desires to know me, one who wants to achieve certain ends, and one who knows me. All these are exalted, but the one who knows Me is considered by Me to be My very self.

Lord Kṛṣṇa says that all these devotees are dear to Him, for all appreciate His presence and power; but *jñānī*, the one who is wise, is the greatest devotee, for only he has the proper knowledge of the Lord.

The statement, "The Lord is", is an expression of *jñānā*, but the sentence, "I am the Lord," expresses *vijñāna*, complete knowledge. Knowing that the Lord exists and that He is the cause of everything is only *jñānā*, but seeing that the Lord is I, Awareness, is *vijñāna*, Awareness is the same in both the Lord and in Me, so in Me is the Lord.

The wave that knows that it is water can say, "I am the ocean; water is the essence of me and of all other waves and of the ocean that has created us." This is complete knowledge, *vijñāna*. The Lord says, "The *jñānī* is the one whose devotion is fulfilled, for that person has become one with Me, by knowledge. A *jñānī* is indeed Myself."

What Is Brahman?

By this time Arjuna has heard Lord Kṛṣṇa use a number of words the meaning of which is unclear to him, and so we find that the eighth chapter begins with a question. Arjuna asks the Lord the meaning of *brahman*, *adhyātma*, and *karma*, among others.

In Sanskrit the meaning of a word is based on the verbal root from which it is derived by well-defined rules of grammar. These roots are in current use; they are not merely of etymological interest. For example, in English, the etymology of the word "world" is obscure, so that the word itself does not reveal its meaning. In Sanskrit, the word for world is "*jagat*", derived from the roots *jan*, to be born, and *gam*, to go, two roots well known by even a beginner in Sanskrit. The meaning of the word *jagat* is, therefore, "that which is born and which then goes"; the word itself describes the transient nature of the world.

We are familiar with the word *brahman;* we translate it as "absolute reality," even though we may not know what is meant by either absolute or reality. "*Brahman*" is a noun derived from the root *bṛh*, to increase, to grow large. The noun means "bigness"

In the study of grammar, we are taught that adjectives qualify nouns, but you will find that nouns also qualify adjectives. If I say that a mountain is big, you visualise a certain size. If I use the same adjective for a building, as in "big building", the big means only "building-big", not "mountain-big". If I want to see a big microbe, I need a microscope. The adjective "big" remaining the same, its dimension changes as the noun it qualifies changes. Thus the noun also qualifies the adjective.

If I form a noun from the root *bṛh*, it means "bigness". Nothing qualifies or limits that bigness; it is unconditionally big. It has no form, no limitation whatsoever. *Paraṁ brahma,* limitless *brahma*, is not limited by space or time, and that is indeed *adhyātma*, or *ātmā*, the existence, consciousness, fullness that is the truth of the individual. The word *ātmā* is resolved as: *āpnoti, vyāpnoti sarvaṁ iti ātmā* — that which pervades everything is called *ātmā*. Thus *ātmā*, Self, is *brahman*, limitless. God and the individual are only apparently two entities; behind both is *paraṁ brahma,* which is *akṣara*, changeless, deathless — and that is the Self. In the eighth chapter, the Lord says, "He who knows himself to be not different from Me, he is one with Me. He is wise and is liberated from birth and death. "

Differences Are Only Apparent

There is no real difference between God and the *jīva*; only their *veśas*, costumes, differ. On the stage one person plays a beggar, another a king; while the king commands respect and obedience, the beggar and his language evoke pity. But there is no beggar or king in the greenroom; both are actors earning the same wages. Similarly, the Lord is the whole creation while you and I are only limited beings. Because of our costumes, we appear to be different. In His role of *īśvara*, the Lord's body is all-pervasive; He is all power, all knowledge. In your role as a *jīva*, you are limited in power, knowledge and other respects. These appearances do not represent real differences. The limitations belong to the body and not to the Self that is of the nature of Awareness.

You are awareness that is not limited; your physical body is only an apparent limitation. One whose mind is awake to this fact is identical with the Lord. Many people criticize

Vedanta because they are incapable of grasping this vision. Vedanta is knowledge of what is and not what appears to be. When you look at yourself in a concave or a convex mirror, you don't become alarmed at the distortion that you see — you know it is only apparent. Similarly, you can play the role of a beggar on the stage but not suffer as the beggar even when the play is performed. The Lord tells Arjuna that one should contemplate upon this teaching until this vision is clear:

अभ्यासयोगयुक्तेन चेतसा नान्यगामिना ।
परमं पुरुषं दिव्यं याति पार्थानुचिन्तयन् ॥ ८-८ ॥

Abhyāsayogayuktena cetasā nānyagāminā
Paramaṁ puruṣaṁ divyaṁ yāti pārthānucintayan (VIII:8)

Contemplating with a mind that is endowed with the capacity to think of Me alone and which does not think of any other object, one reaches that limitless, effulgent Lord.

Death and Birth : Saṁsāra Cakra

Nothing in this world really ends. Matter does not get destroyed, nor does energy. One form may get converted into another, but it does not disappear altogether. There is no logical basis of thinking that the conscious being comes to an end.

You are a conscious being, *jīva,* who is wielding this body-mind complex. The conscious being does not die when the body, which is matter, dies and disintegrates. The scripture says that *jīva* is a traveller, leaving one body and assuming another. Death means only that the association of *jīva* with a given physical body has come to an end. When *jīva* assumes a human body, he or she performs good and bad actions which give rise to good and bad results. Some of the results terminate in this lifetime; others do not. Those unconsumed results — both *puṇya,* virtue, and *pāpa,* sin — will have to be inherited some time in the future; until that time, they remain "on account" for the *jīva.* According to this *puṇya-pāpa* "account", *jīva* gains another body in which he or she performs actions, accumulating more *puṇya* and *pāpa,* which will cause him or her to assume yet another body. In this way, *jīva* keeps moving; this is saṁasāra-*cakra*, the wheel of birth and death. If *jīva* thinks he or she is *saṁsārī*, a person caught in this cycle, it is because of this single error: "I am a doer; the results of action belong to me."

If you know you are actionless, how can you perform action and how can the results ever come to you? When one appreciates that one's nature is actionless, all *puṇya* and *pāpa* standing in one's "account" is written off, for there is no longer a doer to reap those results. There is no rebirth for that wise person, for there is no *puṇya-pāpa* to inherit, and therefore no cause for taking another body.

Some welcome death in the hope that by death, they will put an end to their problems; but death does not release anyone from problems. One only moves on to the next birth and death in this ephemeral world of sorrow. You are born crying, and you continue to cry, moving from sorrow to sorrow until the day you die. *Saṁsāra* is not a merry-go-round. You remain in it until you understand that your nature is actionlessness, that you are not bound by action and its results.

Ending Saṁsāra through Knowledge

Knowing that the Lord and you are the one actionless Awareness, you reach the Lord without effort, for the Lord is yourself.

अनन्यचेताः सततं यो मां स्मरति नित्यशः ।
तस्याहं सुलभः पार्थ नित्ययुक्तस्य योगिनः ॥ ८–१४ ॥

Ananyacetāssatataṁ yo mam smarati nityaśaḥ
Tasyāhaṁ sulabhaḥ pārtha nityayuktasya yoginaḥ

(VIII:14)

I am easy to reach, O Partha, for that *yogī* who remembers Me always, who thinks of nothing but Me.

You think you have lost your purse and search everywhere for it. When you realize that it is in your pocket, is there any difficulty in reaching it? Knowledge of yourself as the limitless being is not an action to be accomplished by you; there is no effort, no motion required. You need not so much as contract your muscles, there is no need to do any *yogāsanas*, no techniques are involved. You only have to recognize yourself as limitless. The Lord says, "One who appreciate Me rightly, who does not miss himself, for him I am *sulabha*, easy to reach.

"One who wants this and that, who is only interested in achieving small ends, will not reach Me. Through paths, one cannot reach Me. You can reach ends by paths, but you cannot cut a path to reach yourself. There are various techniques to make your mind purer, more abiding, subtler: but the real goal is not merely to improve the mind — it is to recognise yourself. For that there is no path. "

Darkness cannot meet light; as light comes, darkness goes. Similarly, ignorance and knowledge are opposed to each other. The Lord says, "I am the easiest to reach as I am the most difficult. If you search for Me, you cannot find Me. But for one whose mind is ready, who has the blessing of teaching, I am easy to know. "

13
King Among Secrets

The eighth chapter of the Gita gives the definition of *brahman* as that which is imperishable, which is limitless, which is not limited by space, time and qualities. Only Awareness, I, is limitless. All things you know are objects of your knowledge and you are a knower with reference to them; but with reference to yourself, you are knowledge — not knowledge of any object, but pure knowledge, the content of any particular knowledge, pure Awareness that has no form. Therefore, Awareness is free from the limitation of time or space or quality. Awareness is *brahman; ayamātmā brahma: Ā tmā* is Awareness, it is *brahman.* This is the message of all the Upaniṣads.

You take yourself to be a limited being, a mortal. Although the physical body, sense organs, and mind are objects of your knowledge, you throw all their limitations upon the *ātmā*, I. You cannot stand limitations and go about trying to remove them; this groping is called *saṁsāra.*

The problem of limitation being illegitimate, cannot be solved by eliminating thoughts — as in *samādhi* — or by raising the *kuṇḍalinī* or by an other action. You remove a given thought or desire, and many more crop up like the heads of a hydra-headed monster. Unless you destroy ignorance, the cause of the problem, the problem will not go. The darkness of ignorance can only be removed by the light of knowledge.

King among Branches of Knowledge

In the ninth chapter of the Gita, knowledge of the Self is called *rāja-vidyā,* king among the branches of knowledge. Diciplines of knowledge are many: alchemy, astrology, astronomy, botany, chemistry, logic, linguistics, and so on. The scope of each discipline is so vast that no one individual can have the last word in even one of these fields; therefore society needs people who specialise in them. There must be someone who knows how to make an automobile, another one who knows what goes into the making of a rocket. A lawyer with a medical problem needs a doctor, and a doctor in legal trouble needs a lawyer. Thus *parasparaṁ bhāvayantaḥ*, helping each other, we live.

Among all branches of knowledge, however, there is one that everyone must know, knowing which one becomes tall beyond measurement. That is the knowledge of you, the one who goes about gaining every other kind of knowledge. It is a waste of human life, if one does not discover the truth about oneself. You may conduct your affairs efficiently, but if you don't know the self, you will always be a confused person, confusing everyone else. Hence the Lord says that the knowledge of the self must be gained. The results of this knowledge are so great that your life is completely changed by it. This knowledge is not within the scope of choice; you must know yourself.

The following question occurs in Muṇḍakopaniṣad:

कस्मिन्नु भगवो विज्ञाते सर्वमिदं विज्ञातं भवतीति ।
—मुण्डकोपनिषद् १-१-३

Kasminnu bhagavo vijñāte sarvamidaṁ vijñātaṁ bhavatīti
(Muṇḍakopaniṣad I:I:3)

Knowing which, O Revered Sir, does everything (as well) become known?

Knowledge of one object will not give you the knowledge of another; knowledge of a pot will not give you the knowledge of cloth. Here it is said that when *brahman*, which is the truth of you and of God, is known, everything as well is known. How can that be?

Know the Lord

The Lord says, "If you know Me you know the whole world, for I am the cause of all creation". The *upādāna kāraṇa*, material cause, of any creation sustains that creation and obtains throughout it. The Lord is the material cause of the whole universe. He says, "*Mayā tatamidaṁ sarvaṁ:* By Me the whole creation is pervaded." Therefore, knowing the Lord, everything as well is known.

But the Lord also says, "The creation is not me." How is this possible? Each and every wave is water. While a wave has no independent existence — it depends entirely upon water — water can be totally independent of the wave. If water were only a wave, wherever water existed it would be in the form of a wave. Water, the material cause of the wave, obtains in the wave and sustains the wave, but is not wave.

So too, the Lord is not creation, even though the creation is pervaded by the Lord. That one thing because of which the creation comes into being, by which it is sustained, and into which it will resolve is *paraṁ brahma,* which is limitless existence, Awareness. There is no question of anything being apart from that.

Know Thyself

Consider an objective creation, a silver chain. The chain did not exist before it was made, but the material, silver, was there. After the chain is made, silver still exists. If the chain is broken or melted, the chain will be gone, but silver will still remain. If silver exists before the chain was made, after the chain is broken, and in between, too, where is the chain? Imagine that a man knows what silver is but does not know what a chain is and wants to see one. You show him the chain, but he will call it silver. A chain consists of links and every link is nothing but silver. Where then is the chain? He recognises only silver. You have to accept that he is right; there is no reality, except silver, for the word 'chain'. It is only by common consent that we call the object a chain. Chain is therefore only the name for a particular form.

Any creation is only *nāma,* a name given to a *rūpa,* a form. The creation itself is like a great magic trick. What is available for public knowledge and handling, what is presented to everybody's perception is *īśvara sṛṣṭi,* the creation of the Lord. We all perceive this world. Upon this, which is objective creation, you project your private opinions and values and see a different world which is your private subjective creation; it is called *jīva sṛṣṭi,* creation of the individual which you alone see. The Lord says, "I am the Lord", and you say "I am the individual"; both enjoy one thing in common:

I...I...I. This I is *brahman,* which is one limitless Awareness. The Lord and I are one Awareness, and from that Awareness alone both the objective and the subjective creations have come. What is projected by your mind and what is projected by the Lord — both are from one Awareness alone.

Real and Apparent : The Great Secret

Does *brahman* really undergo any intrinsic change to become the world? To answer this, let us go back to the silver chain. In becoming the chain or in being the chain, has silver undergone any change? If silver has undergone a change to become the chain, the chain is no more silver but something else. Clay does not undergo a change to become a pot; water undergoes no change even though waves are born. Without undergoing any intrinsic change, things are born. If an effect is created without any intrinsic change in the cause, the change is only apparent. The effect can enjoy a different name and form, but in reality it is the same as the cause. Thus the apparent chain has its reality in silver, the wave in water, and the pot in clay. Clay is real; the pot is apparent. The pot exists when clay exists, but when the pot is gone, clay still remains.

One exists when the other exists; but even when one does not, the other exists. This is an amazing phenomenon. In the ninth chapter of the Gita this is called *rājaguhya,* king among secrets. Now follow this carefully. You are the limitless Awareness; limitless Awareness *is,* and therefore the Lord *is,* the world *is,* your own appreciation of the world *is* — whether your appreciation is proper or not, your desire *is,* the object of your desire *is,* all that exists *is.* All these exist in Awareness. So Lord Kṛṣṇa says,"*Matsthāni sarvabhūtāni:* All things exist in Me alone." Understand what this means: all exist in Me. This is the greatest secret; the Lord is the I.

With the Lord you can say, "All things exist in me alone." This vision is not from the standpoint of your body but from the standpoint of pure Awareness which is your nature. The world *is,* you *are,* the world goes away, you still *are.* In sleep, the world goes away but you still get up and say that you slept. Awareness itself is not affected by these changes; hence, the Lord says, "*Na ca matsthāni:* And, nothing exists in Me."

These statements reveal the nature of the relationship

between the timeless and the time-bound, the infinite and the finite, the absolute and the relative.

As an actor, you may be a king in one movie, a *sannyāsi* in another, a minister in a third. All these beings are in you. These are various roles played by you, the actor; but you are not the king, nor the *sannyāsi,* nor the minister. With reference to these relative roles, you are the absolute, the one who plays all roles, in whom each role has its existence. From your own standpoint, you are independent of all roles. This is what the Lord means by *matsthāni* and *na ca matsthāni.* From your own standpoint, from the standpoint of *ātmā* you are Awareness in which the creation exists but which itself is free from the entire creation. The difference between you, the limitless Awareness, and you, the limited individual, is the difference between the real and the apparent. Silver is real and the chain is apparent. Similarly, you shine independently; everything else is dependent on your existence. Therefore, Lord Kṛṣṇa says, "Arjuna, you are not what you think you are. In fact, you are the opposite. You think you are limited, but in you the whole creation exists."

This is the great secret. Generally a secret can be pried open and let out, but this secret cannot be exposed or discovered by your own efforts, because it is you. Like the person searching for the tenth man you cannot find yourself as long as you are searching for yourself.

For a person who has been taking himself or herself as limited in all possible ways, the truth of this teaching is a secret. If you feel that you are a victim of circumstances, it is because you think that you are limited and the world is real. The world will definitely impinge upon you as a result of this notion, and you will think the world is too much for you. In reality, you are the centre of creation; you *are,* and the creation *is* because of you. How can it hurt you?

You Are Full

When a pot is made, the pot-space (the space enclosed by the pot) does not have to elbow out an area in space to make room for itself. Space is in and through the pot, and is not restricted by walls; it will accommodate everything, and still remain one limitless space. Similarly, I, Awareness, sustains everything. The fullness of that I is described in this line:

अन्तः पूर्णो बहिःपूर्णः पूर्णकुम्भ इवार्णवे ।

Antaḥ pūrṇo bahiṣpūrṇaḥ pūrṇakumbha ivārṇave

A pot filled with water and submerged in the water of the ocean is full inside and outside.

Inside the pot is water; outside too is water. The pot is full inside and outside. Similarly, I is Awareness that is whole, that is fullness. Thoughts come and go, objects of thought come and go, but I, Awareness, is not affected, just as the ocean is not divided by the walls of the submerged pot. If I, Awareness, takes itself to be a thought, anything can affect it, its mind will react. But I is not its thoughts; I is Awareness, fullness, silence. Let objects of perception come; Awareness, I, is not affected by them. I is independent, silence, Awareness. Because of I everything exists.

This knowledge turns the tables on you. Instead of depending on things for your happiness, you know that you are in reality a full, complete being, in whom all things exist. The world exists, you do, the world does not, yet you do. Therefore, the I becomes real, and the world depends upon that I. That which has no independent existence is called *mithyā*. I is *satya*, real, and the world is *mithyā*, apparent; appreciate this simple truth about yourself. Describing this relationship between the world and I, Lord Kṛṣṇa says:

मत्स्थानि सर्वभूतानि न चाहं तेष्ववस्थितः ॥ ९-४ ॥
न च मत्स्थानि भूतानि पश्य मे योगमैश्वरम् ॥ ९-५ ॥

Matsthāni sarvabhūtāni na cāhaṁ teṣvavasthitaḥ (IX:4)

Na ca matsthāni bhūtāni paṣya me yogamaisvaraṁ (IX:5)

All beings have their being in Me, but I do not exist in them.
In Me the beings do not exist. See My glory.

This is the greatest magic; the magician is the Lord, and that Lord is you. Without undergoing any change, you, the Lord, have produced the whole creation, and it will resolve in you again. The Lord says:

राजविद्या राजगुह्यं पवित्रमिदमुत्तमम् ।
प्रत्यक्षावगमं धर्म्यं सुसुखं कर्तुमव्ययम् ॥ ९-२ ॥

Rājavidyā rājaguhyaṁ pavitramidamuttamaṁ
Pratyakṣāvagamaṁ dharmyaṁ susukhaṁ kartumavyayaṁ

(IX:2)

This is the king of knowledge, the king of all secrets, the most exalted of things that purify, that which can be known directly. It is in keeping with dharma, it is most easy to attain, and its result cannot be destroyed.

This most sacred among the secrets is easy to learn for one who is prepared, but most difficult for one who is not ready for this knowledge. So Lord Kṛṣṇa again advises Arjuna how to prepare himself for a life of study.

The Cares of Humankind

The Lord says, "Even if you cannot follow the teaching given to you so far, you can do something to reach your goal".

अनन्याश्चिन्तयन्तो मां ये जनाः पर्युपासते ।
तेषां नित्याभियुक्तानां योगक्षेमं वहाम्यहम् ॥ ९-२२ ॥

Ananyāścintayanto māṁ ye janāḥ paryupāsate
Teṣāṁ nityābhiyuktānāṁ yogakṣemaṁ vahamyahaṁ

(IX:22)

For those people who worship Me, contemplating Me, desiring nothing other than Me, those who are constantly engaged in contemplation, I will take care of their *yoga* and *kṣema.*

With these words the Lord makes this offer to Arjuna: "If you have not understood this teaching it is because your mind is riddled with likes and dislikes; you have to be freed from their hold. Hand over your life to Me. Appreciate Me as the one who is the cause of everything and the *karma phala dātā,* the one who gives the results of action. It is given to you to act, but I give the result. Whether you recognise Me or not, I will give you what your actions deserve. Take the results as they come. When you perform action, think of Me; when the work is over, think of Me. I will take care of your *yoga and kṣema.*"

Anything that you want to accomplish in your life can be categorised as *yoga or kṣema. Yoga* is defined as *aprāptasya prāpaṇam:* achieving what you do not have is *yoga.* A man is unhappy because he has been working to achieve something but has not been able to. This is a problem of *yoga. Kṣema* is defined as *prāptasya rakṣanam:* the protection of what you already have is *kṣema.* A person is sorrowful because his son has met with an accident. This is a problem of *kṣema.* There is no third source of sorrow in life. Either we want something or we do not want to lose what we already have. The life of a *saṁsārī* is spent in the pursuit of *yoga* and *kṣema.* The Lord assures Arjuna that He would take care of both these needs for those who have handed themselves over to Him and who recognise Him as the giver of the fruits of action.

This appreciation of the Lord as the *karma phala dātā* is still a part of Indian culture. The Lord gives the fruits of action, even to those who don't recognise Him, but not knowing this they think that they are carrying the burden of *yoga* and *kṣema* on their shoulders. They are like the person who was carrying a load on his head while riding a camel, thinking that he was saving the camel from carrying the load.

Don't suffer needlessly; recognise that all results come from the Lord and are proper. With this attitude, likes and dislikes can be neutralized and what has been said — all are in Me, yet nothing is in Me — will be very clear. As your mind becomes clearer, freed from reactions, you will discover yourselves as someone on whom the whole creation depends. This is not a transformation involving any becoming or change; it is only giving up ignorance. This is *rājaguhya,* king among secrets, the secret concealed by yourself, in yourself.

The Gita unfolds this vision, and this is the vision of the Upaniṣads also. *Tat* is that limitless, free Self that you want to be; *tat tvaṁ asi:* That thou art. This is the king of secrets.

14

The Glories of the Lord

The Lord has revealed what needs to be revealed, but the problem of not being able to see clearly remains for Arjuna. It has already been said, "If you are unable to appreciate this, you must purify your mind. Perform action, seeing that the results follow My laws. This is the only means of neutralising likes and dislikes. By *karma yoga* you will gain a mind that is poised, a mind capable of learning."

A Peaceful Mind

It has been said before:

ज्ञेयः स नित्यसन्न्यासी यो न द्वेष्टि न काङ्क्षति ॥ ५-३ ॥

Jñeyassa nityasannyāsī yo na dveṣṭī na kāṅkṣati

(V:3)

The one who neither hates nor desires is to be known as *sannyāsi*, a renouncer.

The wise does not surrender to likes and dislikes. One who has knowledge of the limitless Self does not experience ups and downs with the coming and going of things in one's life. Wisdom brings poise.

It sounds as though Lord Kṛṣṇa says that poise is necessary in order to gain knowledge, and knowledge is necessary to gain poise. This is not a vicious circle. The meaning is: To possess absolute poise, you must first have relative poise. If you want to be all peace, you must first be relatively peaceful. A relatively silent mind will discover the silence that is your nature; a relatively peaceful mind will discover the peace that is your nature; a relatively sympathetic mind will discover the sympathy that is your nature. One cannot discover peace through a life of agitation. One begins by cultivating a value for relative peace, a peace that can be brought about by the attitude of *karma yoga.* A mind that enjoys this relative peace can discover absolute, abiding peace through knowledge of the Self. See the difference between these two: you are peace; your mind is peaceful. In the second sentence, peace is an adjective, whereas in the first it is a noun — it is you. The Lord advises Arjuna to cultivate the right attitude and develop a peaceful mind, because to the extent that the mind is peaceful, it is open to teaching.

Sensitive Mind

We often hear the term *antaḥkaraṇa-śuddhi,* purification of the mind. What does this mean? Purification of the mind means the removal of reactions caused by likes and dislikes that occur in the mind. Everyone has them in plenty. Human beings are given the faculty of choice; nature does not programme us to act in a particular way. Using our free will, we choose, picking up likes and dislikes in the process. A child grows up with likes and dislikes, sometimes very finely tuned ones. You cannot bring up a child to have no likes and dislikes, because the child does not have the wisdom to avoid them. As one matures, education, culture, and civilisation create even finer likes and dislikes. In some people, likes and dislikes are gross, in some they are very subtle. Poets, artists and scientists have a high degree of sensitivity because of which they are able to see more than meets the eye of the common observer. This sensitivity can become a problem, because the more sensitive one is, the more vulnerable one becomes to the power of likes and dislikes. To be upset, such a person doesn't require a calamity; even a change of weather brings a frown to his or her face, if the sensitivity he or she enjoys is not supported by strength. If one is sensitive, one must also have a cushion to absorb one's reactions to things that are not exactly as one wishes them to be. A mind that is not supported by such a cushion of attitude and understanding cannot be strong.

How to Change One's Attitude

A man loves a woman and decides to marry her. On the eve

of their marriage he is told that as a child his bride-to-be was lost at a big festival and that she was brought up by foster parents. He remembers that his own sister was lost at that festival long ago, and upon inquiring further finds out that the woman he is planning to marry is his own lost sister. His attitude towards her immediately changes; he now regards her as a sister, not wife.

This change in attitude is brought about by knowledge. Any amount of entreaty by others to think of her as his sister would not have brought about this change, but at best only conditioned him to suppress his feelings for her. When he discovers beyond any doubt that the woman he regarded as his wife-to-be is really his sister, his attitude is truly changed.

So too, a sensitive mind which is told to develop a cushion against reaction can do so only if that cushion is one of knowledge, an attitude based on understanding. That attitude is *prasāda buddhi,* glad acceptance of the results of action as coming from the Lord. For this attitude to be firmly rooted, not just remain a conditioning, one must understand the Lord's glories and see what we as individuals can claim to be our own in this world.

What Do You Own in Life?

In this life, nothing belongs to us. We should always remember that we are visitors on this planet. We were born here but we have come under a visa whose date of expiry is unknown. Since we came, we will go some day.

When we arrived, we brought nothing with us. Each of us was born with a very small physical body, having a certain potential for growth, but we did not bring with us oxygen or food to last for sixty to eighty years. Happily, nature seems to have a perfect understanding of our needs, providing plants to take up our carbon dioxide and give us oxygen to breathe. Thus mutually we can live, helping each other, according to nature's design. It seems we have come to a fully furnished guest house.

You cannot claim authority of anything found in the creation. If you are not the author, you cannot be the owner, the creator is the owner. You cannot say that you created a business empire. To do so, you must first exist, but you did not author your own body. Your business house stands on a piece of land that you did not create. The building that you have there, you did not make. The laws of nature are responsible for the building and the materials with which the building is constructed are drawn from the creation. The brick is not your creation; it was made possible by the Lord who provided the clay. What exactly is your creation?

You cannot name a single thing. Ownership is only a notion.

Think of a person who owns a flat, one of the apartments on the third floor of a five-storey building. She calls it her own house, but let us see what it is she really owns. She does not own the ground on which the building stands, or the floor on which her apartment is located. Even in her own apartment she does not own the floor, for it is the ceiling of the fellow down below. She is not the owner of the ceiling, as that is the floor of the person above her. The left wall happens to be the right wall of her neighbour's apartment and the right wall is naturally the left wall of the other neighbour. She cannot say she owns the space inside her walls. Though she insists that she is the owner, it is not given to her to be the owner of anything.

One can say that one has something, but it is ignorance to say that one owns it. Everything is provided to us. What is it that we have created in this world? One may say that we have made many inventions, but an invention is possible only when there is a potential for it. Going to the moon and returning from it was a possible achievement; going to and returning from the sun is not. Possibilities are provided to us; with our intellect, which has also been provided, we explore, discover, and make use of this world. This is true of any achievement of any age.

The Glories of the Maker

The Lord says in the tenth chapter that any glory which is found anywhere is His. "Since I am the material cause of the entire creation, any glory here is Mine. The wind that blows is Myself; the sun that shines is Myself. I am the wisdom of the wise and the strength of the strong. The voice of a singer is a gift from Me; it has not been created by the singer — she only makes use of it. That the eyes can see, is My glory; that the ears can hear, is My glory. Wherever there is an extraordinary glory, you must see Me there. Although I am everywhere, see Me particularly in these special things: among mountain ranges I am the Himālayas, among peaks I am Everst, among rivers I am the Gaṅgā."

There is no special power that belongs to anyone here; all fame belongs to the Lord. That is why in India great musicians always sing only His glories and not the glories of any mortal being. They recognise that even their singing is His glory. Great sculptors carve only the Lord's forms. Even dance in India is not for getting pleasure nor exercise; it is performed as an offering at the altar of the Lord.

Who Owns Your Body?

No one can claim to own anything, not even one's own body. Your mother has a claim on your body, because she brought it forth and brought it up too; your father has a claim on it because he was its *nimitta kāraṇa*. Your spouse claims that the body belongs to him or her by the sacrament of marriage. Your employer claims it because you are paid for your work. The state has a claim, for as a citizen you have duties to the state. Vegetables, wheat, and rice can also have a claim on your body because they provide nourishment to it; if you are a meat-eater, every goat and chicken can lay a claim on you. The earth has a claim because everything is born of it — and finally it is the earth that will have you. Fire can register a claim because it is fire that maintains the temperature of your body as long as you are alive. Water can register a claim on you because it maintains the shape of your body. The air that you breathe can claim you, the space that accommodates you can claim you. The organisms in your body, of course, have a claim because for generations they have been in your body — it is their home, an inherited one at that. Still a person says, "This is my body!"

Ownership is a notion. You do not own your body nor anything outside it. Even the knowledge that you have gained is not solely authored by you; you received it from many teachers who taught you science, language, mathematics, and so on. You owe to hundreds and thousands of factors and even to the five elements for any achievement. You simply live and enjoy things that are provided for you.

Therefore, the Lord says, "Arjuna, appreciate that everything is My glory."

> यद्यद्विभूतिमत्सत्त्वं श्रीमदूर्जितमेव वा ।
> तत्तदेवावगच्छ त्वं मम तेजोंऽशसम्भवम् ॥ १०–४१ ॥

> *Yadyadvibhūtimatsattvaṁ śrīmadūrjitameva vā*
> *Tattadevāvagaccha tvaṁ mama tejo'ṁśa saṁbhavaṁ*

(X:41)

Whatever is glorious, prosperous or powerful, know it to be but a spark of My glory.

Arjuna is as though being told, "I am your hands, eyes, ears; so where is the question of your claiming anything? When you remember that everything comes from Me, you will find that your mind has become totally different. You are in a world that is provided with everything for your welfare. Having entered therein, enjoy it."

The Cosmic Person

Arjuna then says to the Lord, "I understand that you are the material cause, that you rule the whole creation. I cannot see all your forms at once with these eyes; yet I long to see your cosmic form. Give me some power by which I can see in you the entire creation." The Lord gives Arjuna a special vision by means of which he sees the Lord in His cosmic form, the whole creation in the person of Lord Kṛṣṇa.

You see something as being different from you when you stand apart from the thing and look at it. If you stand apart from yourself, that is from the body-mind complex, you see that you are not that complex — you are Awareness alone and in you the whole creation exists. This is the real cosmic vision, gained through knowledge. By a stroke of the *māyā* of Lord Kṛṣṇa, Arjuna gains this vision. He sees in the Lord the whole creation: he sees himself; he sees beautiful things and frightful things too; he sees Bhīṣma, Droṇa, and others in the jaws of death, crushed in the mouth of Time.

Death accompanies you when you are born. Every wrinkle and grey hair you have is his work. Arjuna sees this handiwork dramatically compressed into a short span of time, and he gets frightened. He begs the Lord to return to His familiar gentle form. "You seem to be one blaze of fire, out to consume the whole world. Please return to your original form, dark, beautiful Kṛṣṇa!"

Having shown Arjuna this vision, the Lord says, "Now you know that there is such a thing as the Total. Don't think that you stand apart from it. See My glories; let your mind, sense organs, and body appreciate Me all the time. The things you see are Me; the power that makes you see is also Me. The more you appreciate this, the more you will find that there is nothing for you to complain about in this beautiful world."

15
Devotion

The first six chapters of the Gita speak mainly of *jīva,* the individual, and the second group of six describe the Lord. The vision of the Gita is that *īśvara,* the efficient and material cause of creation, is not in essence distinct from *jīva.* From the standpoint of the Self, *jīva* and *īśvara* are identical; both are *sat-cit-ānanda,* existence, Awareness, limitlessness.

There is, of course, a difference between the Lord and you in regard to your form. Having only two hands and two legs, you are definitely limited; in contrast, the Lord is whole, comprising all forms. Your form, created by the Lord, is included in His all-pervasive cosmic form. But in regard to the Self, the Lord and you enjoy a common *sat* and *cit.* As the wave and ocean have their being in the same water, you and God are one limitless Awareness.

The Individual and the Total

A wave can regard itself in regard to the ocean, the total, or in regard to the wave, the individual. In regard to the wave, it is limited, born a minute before and soon subject to death. However, even if the wave cannot appreciate itself as water, it can at least appreciate the fact that the ocean is that from which it is born, by which it is sustained, and unto which it returns. Thus, seeing its form included in the ocean, the wave surrenders to its Lord, the ocean.

If, unable to appreciate the common truth of *īśvara* and yourself, you take yourself only as *jīva,* at least strive to appreciate that the *nimitta-upādāna-kāraṇa,* the efficient and material cause of all, is the Lord. This is Lord Kṛṣṇa's advice to Arjuna, at the end of the eleventh chapter:

मत्कर्मकृन्मत्परमो मद्भक्तः सङ्गवर्जितः ।
निर्वैरः सर्वभूतेषु यः स मामेति पाण्डव ॥ ११-५५ ॥

Matkarmakṛnmatparamo madbhaktassaṅgavarjitaḥ
Nirvairassarvabhūteṣu yassa māmeti pāṇḍava (XI:55)

One who performs action for My sake, who holds Me as the final goal, who is devoted to Me, who is free from attachment and without enmity for any being, that one reaches Me, O Arjuna.

Here Lord Kṛṣṇa advises the devotee who is not able to understand that the truth of the Lord is the truth of the self. Such a devotee is advised to act like a *bhṛtya,* an obedient servant who performs every action according to the will of his master, rather than according to his own personal dislikes and likes. This example is called *svāmī-bhṛtya-nyāya,* the master-servant analogy.

In a duty-based society, each person does his or her duty, thereby avoiding disharmony and working to the best of his or her ability. This automatically assures the rights of others. Each citizen works with humility, understanding his or her responsibilities to the community. If you see your presence in society not as an unfortunate accident but as a logical incident, you will find yourself important and approach life with a purpose. If you focus on only a segment of life, you may find reasons to condemn yourself and complain about others; but if your vision is wider, in your understanding of the whole there will be no complaint or condemnation. The Lord says that one's vision should not merely be wider, it should be cosmic. "Take Me into account; know that you are included in My cosmic form. As in your anatomy each cell plays its part, so in the cosmic pattern each individual contributes. If you understand this and perform action, keeping Me in view all the time, you will become *matkarmakṛt,* one who performs actions only for Me."

For one who cannot give up desires and perform action only for the sake of the Lord, Śrī Kṛṣṇa prescribes another approach. "Continue to do your work for achieving what you want; and when the results come, remember Me as the one who gives the fruits of action. One who cultivates this attitude is My devotee; his mind will abide in Me and My teaching will be clear to him."

One who accepts the result of action as *prasāda,* a gift from the Lord, is *nirvaira,* one who has enmity towards none. In the vision unfolded here all beings are part of the whole; you are not an isolated individual. One who appreciates this cannot hate another person, because it is impossible for one to bear enmity towards any part of the totality that includes oneself. If your teeth bite your tongue, you don't knock out your teeth in anger. With this understanding, feelings of restlessness and sorrow will subside, and the cheerful mind will see the truth unfolded by the teaching. Therefore, the Lord says, "*Māmeti:* He will become one with Me", as the wave, discovering "I am water", becomes one with the ocean without undergoing any change.

What Is Devotion?

Having heard this description of *karma yoga,* the yoga of the right attitude towards action, Arjuna asks a relevant question, which opens the twelfth chapter:

एवं सततयुक्ता ये भक्तास्त्वां पर्युपासते ।
ये चाप्यक्षरमव्यक्तं तेषां के योगवित्तमाः ॥ १२-१ ॥

Evaṁ satatayuktā ye bhaktāstvāṁ paryupāsate
Ye cāpyakṣaramavyaktaṁ teṣāṁ ke yogavittamāḥ

(XII :1)

Of those devotees who thus (doing action for Your sake) contemplate you as Lord, and those who contemplate the imperishable, unmanifest Self, who are superior in *yoga?*

The intent of Arjuna's question is: "Is it better that I look upon You as Lord and worship you performing actions for Your sake? Or is it better that I withdraw from the world and contemplate the Self that is *sat-cit-ānanda?* Are those who pursue the truth of the Self better than those who surrender to you and go on doing actions in the world? Which of these will reach You?"

The Lord is amused, because Arjuna has not given up this question of *karma yoga* versus *sannyāsa* since the third chapter. He answers in the next verse, "The one who goes on with his work, not forgetting Me, is better. Why do I say so? If you were ready for *sannyāsa,* you would not ask this question. Since it is necessary for you to ask, I have to say that performance of action is better for you than renunciation."

The question really should not be what is better; it should be what is it that you require. A mind free from likes and dislikes would naturally be drawn to contemplation and would not have this question. A mind which is not contemplative has no choice, because it cannot contemplate. One may sit in an isolated cave for hours, but the mind will not become contemplative. Contemplation, like love, cannot be induced in you. It is something that takes place naturally. Only a mind that has a certain disposition can contemplate. So the Lord says:

मय्यावेश्य मनो ये मां नित्ययुक्ता उपासते ।
श्रद्धया परयोपेतास्ते मे युक्ततमा मताः । १२-२ ॥

Mayyāveśya mano ye māṁ nityayuktā upāsate
Śraddhayā parayopetāste me yuktatamā matāḥ (XII:2)

Those who meditate upon Me, who are steadfast (always doing action for Me), bringing the mind to rest in Me, endowed with great faith, they are the most exalted in My opinion.

In praising those who perform action for His sake, Lord Kṛṣṇa says, "Those who are endowed with great faith and are alert in their thinking will be blessed with freedom. Let your mind dwell in Me; perform actions, but never lose sight of Me. Even when you work to achieve results, remember Me. One who always thinks of Me is not swayed by ego."

Everyone thinks he is the apple of the Creator's eye, the very salt of creation. This I who exults, "No one is equal to me!" is bound to suffer, because another I thinks exactly the same way; and when two egos clash, there is strife, regret, failure, loss of peace and joy.

Recognise that your demand for praise from society is due to ignorance. Appreciate that everything is given to you; you can claim authorship of nothing. Possession in itself is not wrong, but to think "I own things" shows only a lack of appreciation of the Lord who is the author of everything. Thinking of the individual ego makes one small, and with this feeling of smallness one goes about trying to become limitless. To be free from limitation, give up identification with the individual by appreciation of your relationship to the total, the fundamental relationship common to all beings.

The Relative and the Fundamental

Everyone is, from one moment to another, a relative person. Father, husband, son, uncle, master, servant — each one is I, but I is only one, assuming different roles. Each role exists only when there is a particular relationship that evokes it; when objects or individuals change, the role also changes. But among these relationships there is one that does not change. I is related to the total as an individual, to the Creator as the created. This fundamental relationship exists for every being in this world. Whether you like it or not, whether you disavow it or not, every creature in the world and you are related to the Lord.

When you are with your father, you are a son; but when you are with your son, you become a father and the son that you were is gone. Relationship with individuals is thus peculiar and distinct, but is one's relationship to the total, the Lord, distinct and peculiar? You are created, your father is created, your grandfather is created, your uncle, grandson, friend, enemy, mountain, river — all are created and He is the Creator. He is the sustainer, we are the sustained; He is the destroyer, we are the destroyed; He gives the fruits of action, we perform the action; He is the Lord, and we are devotees. Father, son, uncle, friend, enemy — all are devotees. Any role that anybody plays is played only as a devotee. In all your changing roles, you are *jīva* related to the Lord; you are a devotee first and last, a fundamental devotee. With this understanding, how can you ever miss the Lord?

Without this understanding, however, you are a devotee only at the altar. Outside, you are a business person. You are only a spasmodic devotee having bouts of devotion whenever, you are in a temple or a church. If you are fundamentally a devotee, devotion cannot be intermittent.

A cook who has a flare for music is only a cook who sings. If he studies music very well and finally becomes a professional musician whose hobby is cooking, he is a great musician who cooks. See the transformation. When music becomes his life, he is no more an occasional musician; he will discover music in the boiling of water or in the noise of a moving train.

Similarly, an occasional devotee can become a permanent devotee by constant remembrance of the Lord. That is why a temple tower or church steeple is so high — to be constantly in sight, reminding us that the Lord is there in all our thoughts and actions, so that we may all the time gracefully accept His blessing. By cultivating this attitude one comes to command a mind that can receive the knowledge that destroys the *ahaṅkāra,* the notion of an isolated I.

Until one is able to see the Lord always, in all the phenomena and laws of the world, one must cultivate the devotee in oneself by engaging in various forms of worship such as prayers, singing, chanting, rituals, etc. To become a musician, a person practises singing until it becomes natural; the practice is meaningful because singing is the means by which the singer can attain his or her goal of being an accomplished musician. Similarly, all forms of worship become relevant if one understands that worship is the means of becoming a permanent devotee, and that a permanent devotee can discover his or her identity with the Lord.

Invocation and Worship

All worship is aimed at cultivating this attitude, to help bring out the devotee in one. The purpose of offering a coconut to the Lord or doing ritualistic worship is that by these actions the fanciful mind learns to appreciate Him. This is not the worship of an idol. When you invoke the Lord in a form such as a cross or a crescent or a lump of turmeric powder, you are not worshipping that form, but the Lord represented there. Anything you offer goes not to the idol of clay or stone, but to the Lord you invoke.

Day after day people in India go to temples and declare, "All wealth is yours; my body, and my mind belong to you; of all this you are the author and owner, O Lord!" If by these words you really mean to offer all you have to the Lord, what is the need for repeating this every day? Does it mean you are bluffing even in your prayers? Of course it doesn't. This chant is repeated daily so that one can slowly transform oneself into a real devotee, a devotee first and last. The business person who prays can become the devotee who transacts business. When one's relationship to the Lord becomes primary, ali other relationships become secondary and the problems encountered in them are resolved. As a devotee you have no problem; the Lord does not need anything from you.

Devotion Is an Attitude

You may sing His glory in any language, for it is not language that matters; what matters is your understanding and attitude. The Lord says:

पत्रं पुष्पं फलं तोयं यो मे भक्त्या प्रयच्छति ।
तदहं भक्त्युपहृतमश्नामि प्रयतात्मनः ॥ ९-२६ ॥

Patraṁ puṣpaṁ phalaṁ toyaṁ yo me bhaktyā prayacchati
Tadahaṁ bhaktyupahṛtamaśnami prayatātmanaḥ

(IX:26)

What ever is offered to Me with devotion — leaf, flower, fruit, or water, offered by the pure-minded — I take.

Lord Kṛṣṇa tells Arjuna that what is offered is not of consequence; "You may even offer something mentally; that is enough for Me. What is important is only your attitude."

Many people feel that devotion is easy; but it is not. Often respect is not shown and salutations that traditionally are to be offered to elders are not offered, because of *ahaṅkāra,* ego. Similarly, ego often prevents one from expressing devotion to the Lord. A man with a big ego cannot even place a flower at the altar of an idol unless he has at least some appreciation from the Lord. Surrender is not easy. It is not easy to love. To discover devotion one must create a mental condition that is conducive to expressing love for the Lord — at least one must avoid creating conditions that stifle the expression of love.

It is you who stand isolated from the Lord as an iceberg of ego which, though surrounded by its source, water, remains crystallised and separate. Worship the Lord in order to melt away this crystallised ego. Even while you act in order to achieve, remember the Lord when you receive the result of your action. By this you will neutralise your likes and dislikes and your ego will be dissolved. Only then can you discover that He and you are the same. This knowledge of the identity of the Lord and the devotee is the consummation of a life of devotion, for worship helps the devotee to develop a tranquil mind free from wants, a mind that can recognise the truth presented by the teacher and the teaching.

Bhakti, devotion, is defined as:

सा त्वस्मिन् परमप्रेमरूपा ।

—नारदभक्तिसूत्र-२

Sā tvasmin paramapremarūpā (Nārada-bhakti-Sūtra:2)

That (devotion) verily is in the form of supreme love to this (the Lord).

Absolute love resolves duality. Even in the love between two persons, separation ends; the two are fused in emotional identity. If love for the Lord is total, it liquidates the individual. In perfect love or surrender the individual is dissolved in the Lord not like a salt crystal in water, but like water in water. There is only one Lord who expresses the inside and outside of you. The individual is a notion; all is the Lord. You dissolve as the wave dissolves into the ocean; what goes is only your notion — that you are different. It is dissolved in the ocean of knowledge.

Yoga is the Means to Knowledge

To think that the path of *bhakti,* devotion, is better than that of *jñāna,* knowledge, is childish. Total surrender and complete knowledge are identical. In the Gita, the Lord makes no distinction between *bhakti* and *jñāna.* He keeps evading Arjuna's question about which is superior: *karma yoga* or renunciation of action. Since he has likes and dislikes, the *karma yogī* cannot give up *karma,* activity, but he can give up concern for *karmaphala,* the results of action, by cultivating *prasāda buddhi,* the attitude of glad acceptance that all results come from the Lord. Performing action with this attitude brings about purification; that is, he is released from the hold of likes and dislikes. This recognition that the Lord is the giver of all fruits of action is *bhakti.* Thus *karma yoga* is *bhakti,* and it is the means for gaining śānti, peace of mind. A peaceful mind will discover the peace that is one's nature.

The *sannyāsī,* the renouncer, on the other hand, gives up activities and devotes himself completely to the knowledge that the Lord and he are not different. This knowledge is absolute *bhakti.* Thus the goal of both the *karma yogī* and the *sannyāsī* is knowledge of the identity of the Lord and the individual, and that knowledge is absolute devotion.

Which lifestyle to adopt is not a question of choice. A *sannyāsī* has no likes and dislikes, no fear of the world; so for him, renunciation is natural. If you are afraid of the world, you must live in the world and become its master. Then you have a choice of leaving it or remaining in it, but if you want to leave because you cannot live in it, it is better for you to stay. This is an important aspect of the teaching of the Gita and the Lord dwells on this same theme from the second chapter onwards. Although repetition is considered a defect in *vedānta śāstra,* it is accepted in the Gita because it is a teaching in the form of a dialogue between teacher and student, and the Lord's concern is that Arjuna should understand Him. Even after listening to the teaching contained in the second and third chapters, Arjuna does not seem to understand that he would not lose anything by continuing to perform action; so, Lord Kṛṣṇa continues to talk of *karma yoga* from the ninth to twelfth chapters. His message is: "If you cannot appreciate Me as the absolute, think of Me in every action that you perform; treat it as My action, and appreciate Me as the one who gives all the results of action. By this act your mind will become peaceful."

If this is understood, there is no need to ask which is better, a life of devotion, or one of action. In fact, the *yoga* of devotion is the same as that of action, for *bhakti,* devotion, is the very attitude which makes you a *karma yogi,* performing action for the Lord's sake, gladly accepting all results as His blessing. *Karma yoga* is indeed *bhakti yoga.* This is Lord Kṛṣṇa's answer to Arjuna.

16

The Field and the Knower of the Field

The thirteenth chapter begins with a question from Arjuna:

प्रकृतिं पुरुषं चैव क्षेत्रं क्षेत्रज्ञमेव च ।
एतद्वेदितुमिच्छामि ज्ञानं ज्ञेयं च केशव । १३-१ ॥

Prakṛtiṁ puruṣaṁ caiva kṣetraṁ kṣetrajñameva ca
Etadveditumicchāmi jñānaṁ jñeyaṁ ca keśava (XIII:1) [1]

O Lord, I want to know the meaning of these words: *prakṛti* and *puruṣa, kṣetra* and *kṣetrajña, jñānaṁ* and *Jñeyaṁ.*

The Lord begins his answer:.

इदं शरीरं कौन्तेय क्षेत्रमित्यभिधीयते ॥ १३-२ ॥

Idaṁ śarīraṁ kaunteya kṣetramītyabhīdhīyate (XIII:2)

Arjuna, this body is called *kṣetra.*

The Kṣetra

Anything that falls within one's field of experience is called *kṣetra,* but in His initial statement the Lord speaks only of the body. The Lord's intention is to point out to Arjuna the difference between the field and the knower of the field, *kṣetra and kṣetrajña.* No one takes the objects one perceives as oneself but somehow one does take the physical body as

---

1. In several manuscripts, this stanza is not found. Śaṅkara, for instance, didn't accept it. However, ift completes the 700 stanzas of the Gita.

oneself even though the body is as much an object of knowledge as a pot is. Therefore, Lord Kṛṣṇa omits what is obvious and tells Arjuna, "Because your physical body is an object of your perception, it is *kṣetra*." The Lord then goes on to state that *kṣetra* also includes the entire phenomenal world:

महाभूतान्यहङ्कारो बुद्धिरव्यक्तमेव च ।
इन्द्रियाणि दशैकं च पञ्च चेन्द्रियगोचराः ॥ १३-६ ॥

Mahābhūtānyahaṅkāro buddhiravyaktameva ca
Indriyāṇi daśaikaṁ ca pañca cendriyagocarāḥ (XIII:6)

The five elements (space, air, fire, water, earth), the ego, the intellect, ignorance, the ten organs (the five organs of perception and the five organs of action), the one (the mind) and the five sense objects (sound, form and colour, touch, smell and taste) — all these are *kṣetra*, objects.

Lord Kṛṣṇa's meaning is: "All that you are aware of — all objects, your likes and dislikes, pleasures, misery, fortitude, your knowledge, and ignorance all this is *kṣetra*."

The Kṣetrajña

One who is aware of *kṣetra*, including this physical body and this phenomenal world, is *kṣetrajña*, the knower of *kṣetra*. Who is aware of this physical body and everything that comprises it? Who is aware of the experiences of hunger and thirst, of the various conditions of the mind, of the knowledge of a given thing, of the feeling of being happy or unhappy, of the notion of the doer and the enjoyer? It is *kṣetrajña*, because of whom I become the seer, hearer, smeller, taster, thinker, doubter, knower. In all these roles, the I is common. That I is *kṣetrajña*, limitless Awareness. Śaṅkarācārya writes in Dakṣiṇāmūrti Stotra:

नानाच्छिद्रघटोदरस्थितमहादीपप्रभाभास्वरं...
—दक्षिणामूर्तिस्तोत्र -४

Nānācchidra-ghaṭodara-sthita-mahādīpaprābhā-bhāsvaraṁ...
(Dakṣiṇāmūrti-stortra 4)

Like the radiance of a brightly glowing lamp placed inside a pot that has many holes in it...

Imagine a pot with five holes placed in a room that is dark. One places a light in the pot so that five beams of light emerge, each illumining objects that fall in its path. What lies between the beams will not be illumined: only what falls in their path will be seen. Now think of your physical body as a fragile pot with five apertures, the sense organs: eyes, ears, nose, tongue, and skin. The light that comes out through these apertures, illumining the world, is Awareness. Awareness in your body obtains in your five sense organs. Therefore, the one source of light, Awareness, emerges as five beams of light through the five organs of perception and illumines form and colour through the eyes, sound through the ears, smell through the nostrils, taste through the tongue and touch through the skin. The five beams of light are only one light. That light in you, in me, in everyone, is indeed Awareness that is the Lord. Lord Kṛṣṇa says:

क्षेत्रज्ञं चापि मां विद्धि सर्वक्षेत्रेषु भारत ॥ १३-३ ॥

Kṣetrajñaṁ cāpi māṁ viddhi sarvakṣetreṣu bhārata (XIII:3)

Arjuna, know Me to be the *kṣetrajña* in all beings.

You think that you are different from others because you take your body, intellect, mind, etc., as I; but when you know the nature of that I, you will see that all differences belong to the *kṣetra,* the phenomenal world, and not to you. *Kṣetrajña,* Awareness, indeed is the basis of all forms.

Kṣetrajña Is Jñeyaṁ and Puruṣa

That *kṣetrajña* is *jñeyam,* that which is to be known, to be discovered as I: and that indeed is *puruṣa,* meaning that which is *pūrṇa,* full, and which abides in all beings. Lord Kṛṣṇa says, "Know Me to be the indweller in everybody."

Picture this physical body as a city with sense organs functioning as intelligence officers. There is a *svāmī,* a Lord, who resides in this city and transacts business with the world. That Lord is the *puruṣa,* which is to be known as *paraṁ brahma,* the limitless.

अनादिमत्परं ब्रह्म न सत्तन्नासदुच्यते ॥ १३-१३ ॥

Ānādimat paraṁ brahma na sattannāsaducyate (XIII:13)

Brahman, which is limitless and beginningless, is said to be neither existent nor nonexistent.

From its own standpoint, *brahman,* Awareness, is not limited by space, because It has no form. Everything falls within Awareness, which is not bound by time and space; it is because of Awareness that you are aware of time and space. The *kṣetrajña* is Awareness in which the concepts of time and space — both objective and subjective — exist. Therefore, Awareness is *anādi,* without beginning. It is beyond existence and non-existence. That a man exists is a fact; that he has no horns is also a fact; the one who knows both is *kṣetrajña,* the Awareness because of which you are aware of *sat,* what is, and *asat,* what is not.

All that you perceive is *kṣetra,* the creation. With reference to this creation the Lord, as the material cause, is called *prakṛti, māyā,* or Goddess. The same Lord as the intelligent cause for this creation is called *puruṣa.* The essential reality of the Lord, of *puruṣa* and *prakṛti,* is I, Awareness, *brahman,* which has no gender, form or quality.

With reference to creation, Lord Kṛṣṇa has said earlier, "*Mātsthāni sarvabhūtāni; mayā tatamidaṁ sarvam*: All beings are in Me; by Me everything is pervaded, for I am the material cause of the entire creation." Now He continues, "I am *paraṁ brahma,* the efficient cause of the whole creation." *Brahman* that is beginningless and limitless is the Creator, the *kṣetrajña,* the *puruṣa.* Thus *īṣvara* is *kṣetrajña* and *kṣetra, puruṣa* and *prakṛtī. Puruṣa* is *caitanya,* Awareness, and *prakṛti* is *jaḍa,* inert. Both brought together are *īśvara,* the whole creation. Therefore, in regard to creation:

सर्वतः पाणिपादं तत्सर्वतोऽक्षिशिरोमुखम् ।
सर्वतः श्रुतिमल्लोके सर्वमावृत्य तिष्ठति ॥ १३-१४ ॥

Sarvatah pāṇipadaṁ tat sarvato kṣiśiromukhaṁ
Sarvatah śrutimalloke sarvamāvṛtya tiṣṭhati (XIII:14)

That (which is to be known) has hands and feet everywhere; eyes, heads and mouths everywhere; and ears everywhere. Pervading everything, It abides.

The wave that knows it is water can say, "I am the Atlantic and the Pacific". Similarly, knowing that you are the limitless you can say, "*Sarvataḥ pāṇipādo'ham* : I am the one with hands and feet all over." To the Lord you can say, "I am You, and You are everything. Therefore, I indeed am everything." The beauty of this realization is described in the next verse:

सर्वेन्द्रियगुणाभासं सर्वेन्द्रियविवर्जितम् ।
असक्तं सर्वभृच्चैव निर्गुणं गुणभोक्तृ च ॥ १३-१५ ॥

Sarvendriyaguṇābhāsaṁ sarvendriyavivarjitaṁ
Asaktaṁ sarvabhṛccaiva nirguṇaṁ gunabhoktṛ ca (XIII:15)

That (which is to be known) manifests itself through the functioning of all the organs of perception, but it is free from all of them. Uninvolved, it sustains all creation; free from all experiences, it enjoys all.

I, Awareness, is the one because of whom the sense organs perceive all objects; but at the same time it is free from all sense organs. Electricity can say, "I am all fans, I am all lights, I am all refrigerators; yet I am free from them all." Space can say, "I am everything because I pervade everything, and yet I am free from everything." Only one who is free from all can be all. Because I is all-pervasive, I is not attached to any particular thing; but I is the one from whom everything is born, by whom everything is sustained, and in whom everything resolves. Therefore,

उपद्रष्टानुमन्ता च भर्ता भोक्ता महेश्वरः ॥ १३-२३ ॥

Upadraṣṭānumantā ca bhartā bhoktā maheśvaraḥ (XIII:23)

The I is the witness of all, the one who permits all, the sustainer, the enjoyer, the Supreme Lord.

A street lamp shines, illumining whatever you do in its

light. It is neither happy nor miserable on account of good or bad things that happen under it. So too, I, Awareness, witnesses all and permits all. Awareness does not interfere in your affairs; it allows your mind to do whatever it likes. That is why someone is wise and someone else is not.

Free from qualities, Awareness sustains all qualities. It is *vibhakteṣu avibhaktam,* undivided among divided things, like the space which is undivided, but appears divided because of walls. See the wonder of it. You are undivided but appear divided. You are motionless but appear as though you move. When thoughts move, it appears as though Awareness moves, but Awareness is motionless, for it abides everywhere; it is not confined to a given place. This Awareness is what you really are. This is what is to be known. The Lord says, "You want to know *ātmā* that is *jñeyam.* It is far away for one who seeks it, because the seeker is the sought; but for one who is taught by a teacher, it is very near."

Jñānam : Values for Living

To know this *puruṣa,* the limitless Awareness that you are, you must have a quiet mind. Learning takes place only in a quiet, alert mind, not in a mind buffeted by agitations. Lord Kṛṣṇa enumerates certain values or attitudes that are necessary for the development of a mind, for it to see the truth of the Self. Because these values are a means of gaining *jñānam,* knowledge, they are here called *jñānam.* The word *jñānam* is derived in this way : *jñāyate anena iti jñānam* : that by means of which something is known is *jñānam.*

Lord Kṛṣṇa lists twenty values as means of knowledge. An analysis of everyone of these shows that each one eads to one value: to attain a quiet, abiding mind, to keep you with yourself.

अमानित्वमदम्भित्वमहिंसा क्षान्तिरार्जवम् ।
आचार्योपासनं शौच स्थैर्यमात्मविनिग्रहः ॥ १३-८ ॥
इन्द्रियार्थेषु वैराग्यमनहङ्कार एव च ।
जन्ममृत्युजराव्याधिदुःखदोषानुदर्शनम् ॥ १३-९ ॥
असक्तिरनभिष्वङ्गः पुत्रदारगृहादिषु ।
नित्यं च समचित्तत्वमिष्टानिष्टोपपत्तिषु ॥ १३-१० ॥

मयि चानन्ययोगेन भक्तिरव्यभिचारिणी ।
विविक्तदेशसेवित्वमरतिर्जनसंसदि ॥ १३–११ ॥

अध्यात्मज्ञाननित्यत्वं तत्त्वज्ञानार्थदर्शनम् ।
एतज्ज्ञानमिति प्रोक्तमज्ञानं यदतोऽन्यथा ॥ १३–१२ ॥

Amānitvamadambhitvamahiṁsā kṣāntirārjavam
Ācāryopāsanaṁ śaucaṁ sthairyamātmavinigrahaḥ

Indriyārtheṣu vairāgyamanahaṅkāra eva ca
Janma-mṛtyu-jarā-vyādhi-duḥkha-doṣānudarśanam

Asaktiranabhiṣvaṅgaḥ putradāragṛhādiṣu
Nityaṁ ca samacittatvamiṣṭāniṣṭopapattiṣu

Mayi cānanyayogena bhaktiravyabhicāriṇī
Viviktadeśasevitvamaratirjanasaṁsadi

Adhyātmajñānanityatvaṁ tattvajñānārthadarśanam
Etajjñānamiti proktamajñānaṁ yadato'nyathā (XIII:8-12)

Absence of pride; unpretentiousness; noninjury; accommodation; straightforwardness; service to the teacher; purity; steadfastness; self-restraint; dispassion towards sense objects; absence of egoism; being aware of problems of birth, death, old age, disease and sorrow; freedom from ownership; caring without attachment for son, wife, home and so on; equanimity in meeting the desirable and the undesirable; devotion to the Lord; resorting to a quiet place; absence of craving for company; continuous study of the scriptures that give knowledge of the Self; and seeing the truth of the Self — these are indeed (the means of) knowledge. What is opposed to these is ignorance.

Amānitvam[1] is absence of pride. A man who has an exaggerated opinion of himself is called a *mānī,* and his attitude is *mānitvam,* pride. Absence of *mānitvam* is *amānitvam.* A proud person demands respect; he may possess some good

1. For a detailed discussion on values, see Swamiji's book, *The Value of Values.*

qualities, but he expects others to recognise him for them because he feels insufficient within in spite of his qualities. One cannot be happy with the respect that comes from others in response to demand. If one is respected because of power, that respect will disappear when one's power fades. Respect should be commanded, not demanded. If you are content with yourself, your happiness does not depend on whether others respect you or not. An attitude of humility helps one keep pride away and maintain a peaceful mind.

Adambhitvam is unpretentiousness. He who does not have any special merit but through speech, dress, or actions presents himself as different from what he really is, is called a *dambhī*, his attitude is *dambhitvam,* its absence *adambhitvam.* Presenting yourself as other than what you are will only invite problems; for if you tell a number of lies, you must remember them all to avoid being caught on the wrong foot. If you speak the truth, you need not pose. Admitting one's limitations and not wanting to represent oneself falsely are values that will free one from problems caused by pretensions; the mind remains free from conflicts born of a split personality that knows one thing and represents another.

Ahiṁsā means noninjury. In nature's creation one life depends on another, but deliberate injury beyond one's minimum needs is *hiṁsā,* injury. One who appreciates the sanctity of life and therefore does not consciously injure anyone — *kāyena vācā manasā,* by deed, word, or thought — for one's own benefit, such a person is observing *ahiṁsā* by showing appreciation of the rights and points of view of others, including the plant and animal kingdoms. One must discover this attitude of respect for the rights and requirements of others.

Kṣānti is accommodation of others. You are not happy because you cannot accommodate the other one. You want the other to change rather than change yourself. You don't expect fire to be cold or a scorpion to be without a sting — you just accept their nature and handle them properly or keep away from them; you do not try to change them and then regret because you could not do so. Similarly, people are of many different dispositions. If you can take them as they are, you will enjoy *śānti,* peace. You will be disappointed, if you expect them to change to be exactly what you want them to be.

Everyone has his or her own capacity and problems; the change that you want may not be possible for them. If you understand this, ninety per cent of your problems in relating to people will be solved. Your heart must be commodious; accept the person. If you can help someone change, do so; if you cannot, pray for his or her betterment. The world is wide enough to accommodate the other person; why should your heart be small?

Ārjavam is straightforwardness. When thought, word, and deed are in agreement, their harmony makes you straightforward.

Ācārya-upāsanam means serving the teacher. You completely surrender yourself to the teacher so that you can receive knowledge. This does not mean that you surrender your intellect and blindly accept whatever you are told; by that, you will be allowing yourself to be exploited by anyone. Readiness to serve the teacher represents the right attitude.

Śaucam is purity. You maintain cleanliness inside and outside. Your body, your clothes, your house — all are kept clean, and by being alert about yourself you keep your mind also clean. You don't entertain any ill-will, and if jealousy occurs you nip it in the bud.

Sthairyam means steadfastness. Whatever you are called upon to do by your family or society, country or humanity, you do, holding your mind steady like a sentry holding a post.

Ātmavinigraha means self-restraint, mastery over the mind. When you are deliberate in your thinking, you are not misled by your own thoughts; you are the master of your mind.

Indriyārtheṣu vairāgyam is dispassion towards sense objects, not being a slave to the sense organs. We all fall for advertisements; our likes and dislikes seem to be set by the media, so that we do not have any say in what we pursue. One who is not led by the fancies of the mind has *vairāgyam.*

Anahaṅkāra is absence of egoism. A number of factors are responsible for any achievement. Never think that you have achieved anything all by yourself. Recognition of this fact brings an attitude of *anahaṅkāra*.

Janma-mṛtyu-jarā-vyādhi-duḥkha-doṣānudarśanam is an understanding of the nature of human existence. Death is certain for one who is born. There is no knowing when death will come, but if it waits long enough, old age and disease will visit before it arrives. Accepting these realities, appreciate the marvel that is life. In spite of all the germs in the stomach and all the trucks on the street, one is alive. To be alive to the moment and to make use of it, not letting it pass without one's becoming wiser, takes a certain attitude. One discovers this attitude by inquiry into the facts of human existence.

Asakti is freedom from ownership. You do not own anything, for you are not the author of anything here. Cultivate an attitude that you do not own anything; you just possess a few things.

Anabhiṣvaṅga is an attitude of caring for children, wife, house, and so on, without being attached to them. All these do require a certain amount of care, but remember that you do not own them. If you appreciate the fact that you only possess them temporarily, you will take good care of them. If a friend entrusts you with her car, you take better care of it than you do of your own. Think of yourself not as the owner, but as the managing trustee of your family or home — even of your physical body. Freedom from ownership is *asakti;* the resultant attitude of caring without attachment is *anabhiṣvaṅga.*

Samacittatvam means equanimity of the mind; a poise that is maintained whether you are faced with good or bad, success or failure — in short, the attitude of a *karmayogī*. Equanimity is called *yoga.*

Avyabhicāriṇī bhakti is unswerving devotion to the Lord. Do not take anything, even the elements, for granted. In all these, see the Lord all the time. If you lose sight of Him, you will find that your ego will grow every day.

Vivikta-deśa-sevitvam means resorting to a quiet place. Repair to a quiet place, pull back, pause, and take stock of yourself. This is the purpose of meditation.

Janasaṁsadi arati is absence of craving for company. Do not be afraid of being with people, but do not run after them. Spending time in the company of others can be a form of escape, and every escape is a postponement of seeing what you are. See that you can be happy by yourself.

Adhyātma-jñāna-nityatvam is regular and constant study of the scriptures, of Vedanta. May you study the Gita every day. Do not give up the study, for the more you are in its company, the more you will be in touch with the beauty and the limitlessness that you are.

Tattva-jñānārtha-darśanam is seeing the truth about yourself. Truth, beauty, profundity, limitlessness — these are you. Keep that vision. Appreciate it in contemplation.

These are the values taught to Arjuna by the Lord as the means of gaining knowledge of the Self. You will find that if you are endowed with these, you have everything; you will discover yourself to be what you are seeking. You will know what you are.

17
The Three Qualities

The Gita unfolds the knowledge of *brahman* — the essential nature of the individual, the Lord and the creation. In unfolding this knowledge, the first six chapters talk mainly of the individual, while the next six chapters deal with the Lord, ending with a discussion on *bhakti*, devotion to the Lord. The last six chapters talk of the identity between the individual and the Lord. In the thirteenth chapter, the Lord says, "I am *brahman*, the one that is to be known. I am indeed the conscious Self in all beings, *kṣetrajña*, the one who is aware of the body-mind complex and the world outside." The teaching presented in this chapter makes clear the identity of *kṣetrajña* and *kṣetra*, and in this identity the individual and the total are resolved.

One might wonder: If *brahman* associated with *māyā* is the cause of everything, how is it that everyone is not similar? When the cause is one, why should the effects be varied? The body-mind complex of a human being is nothing but *prakṛti*, matter, vivified by *caitanya*, conscious-ness. *Prakṛti* and *caitanya* being the same in everyone why should one person be contemplative, another ambitious, and a third dull? The fourteenth chapter, called *Guṇatraya-vibhāga-yoga*, the chapter on the Three Qualities, accounts for these differences.

By observing the nature of creation we can appreciate the nature of its cause, for the nature of the cause must inhere in its effects. By examining a fabric you can infer the quality of the cotton from which it is made.

All the constituents of creation can be classified into three categories called *guṇas*, qualities: *sattva*, related to knowledge; *rajas*, related to activity; and *tamas*, related to inactivity. Since these qualities are seen in the creation, we can infer that they exist in its cause, *prakṛti*, so that everything that comes from *prakṛti* — including the psychological disposition of a given individual — is characterised by these three *guṇas*.

The Lord says that everyone is a mixture of these three *guṇas,* but the predominance of one *guṇa* over the other two accounts for the dissimilarities observed among people. A person in whom *sattva* is predominant will be contemplative, for *sattva-guṇa* accounts for peacefulness, knowledge, inquiry and clear thinking. Such a person is *sattva-guṇa-pradhāna,* having *sattva* as the predominant quality, and is called a *brāhmaṇa* by quality. He or she is contemplative as a result of *sattva,* but still sufficiently active because he has *rajas;* and of course he or she also yawns and goes to sleep under the influence of *tamas.*

Rajas accounts for activity. One who is hyperactive, ambitious, out to accomplish something, who can be easily touched to the quick, is predominantly influenced by *rajas.* If *sattva* is next to *rajas* in predominance, the person will be active but thinking, and his activities will not be self-centred; he or she will be wedded to an ideal. Such a person may win laurels for his or her work, but in the process, society will also be benefited. This type of person is called a *kṣatriya* by quality.

If, on the other hand, *tamas* occupies the second place in a person in whom *rajas* is predominant, that person will be active but generally selfish or greedy, the type of business person who charges even for a smile given to a customer. This type, called a *vaiśya* by quality, is likely to reap sorrow from his or her activities.

A fourth type of person is generally dull, becoming active only now and then to satiate his or her urges. In such a person, the predominant quality is *tamas,* followed by *rajas*; he or she is called a *śūdra* by quality.

Thus there are four types of people: *brāhmaṇa, kṣatriya, vaiśya* and *śūdra,* differing in the proportion of *sattva, rajas* and *tamas* in their make-up. You should note that although these names are also the names of the four castes, they refer here to the quality of a person's disposition and not to his or her caste by birth. These four kinds of people are found all over the world, not only in India. Everyone is born with *tamas* predominant; a newborn baby sleeps twenty hours a day. As it grows, it sleeps less and becomes more active, comes more under the influence of *rajas.* As it accumulates knowledge, it becomes more and more shaped by *sattva.* When one is able to see in things more than meets the eye, to go beyond the sense organs to see the profundity of life, one is *sāttvika*; influenced by *sattva*; one is then contemplative.

Everyone must grow to be *sāttvika.* To do this, one who is *tāmasa*-whose predominant activity is eating and sleeping — has to become *rajasa,* active, first; even if his actions are selfish at first, he must begin to do something. Afterwards his activity can be gradually turned towards work dedicated to a cause other than fulfilling his own needs. In this process, if he does not abuse his intellect, he will become more and more *sāttvika.*

All the three qualities are found in every *antaḥkaraṇa,* mind; everyone is at times contemplative, at times active and at times dull. The predominance of one of the three accounts for one's peculiar disposition. An animal is predominantly *tāmasa,* not thinking, but led by instincts; whereas a human being is blessed with the faculty of reason, and through this has the potential of developing a *sāttvika* disposition. A person with such a disposition is capable of inquiry and contemplation leading to the solution of the fundamental human problem of ignorance.

The Lord says:

नान्यं गुणेभ्यः कर्तारं यदा द्रष्टानुपश्यति ।
गुणेभ्यश्च परं वेत्ति मद्भावं सोऽधिगच्छति ॥ १४–१९ ॥

Nānyaṁ guṇebhyaḥ kartāraṁ yadā draṣṭānupaśyati
Guṇebhyaśca paraṁ vetti madbhāvaṁ so'dhigacchati

(XIV : 19)

When the wise man sees that the doer is not other than the *guṇas* and knows that which is beyond the *guṇas,* he attains My nature.

The one who knows that it is only the mind that performs all actions — that actions are the work of the *guṇas* that shape the mind and also knows the Self that vivifies the mind that enjoys these *guṇas* — he knows Me. He is not subject to sorrow or delusion because he is not under the spell of the *guṇas* which are the cause of sorrow and delusion. He knows that he is that which transcends the *guṇas,* that stands as the witness illumining the mind. If the mind is restless or frightened he does not think that he is restless or frightened. He does not take himself to be the doer of action or the enjoyer of its fruits. These roles belong to the mind. He knows, "I am like a theatre lamp, illumining everything that happens on the stage of life. All the distinctions seen here are apparent and I alone am the Truth." He knows that he is indeed *īśvara*, who is the creation and is also free from the creation. The Lord says, "That one becomes one with Me.

18

The Tree of Saṁsāra

All the apparent differences in creation that Lord Kṛṣṇa
carefully accounts for in the previous chapter are resolved in
the fifteenth chapter. The chapter begins with a description
of the tree of saṁsāra:

ऊर्ध्वमूलमधःशाखमश्वत्थं प्राहुरव्ययम् ।
छन्दांसि यस्य पर्णानि यस्तं वेद स वेदवित् ॥ १५-१ ॥

Ūrdhvamūlamadhaśśākhamaśvatthaṁ prāhuravyayaṁ
Chandāṁsi yasya parṇāni yastaṁ veda sa vedavit

(XV:1)

They speak of the indestructible *aśvattha* tree that has its
root above and branches below. Its leaves are the Vedas.
The one who knows that tree knows the Vedas.

Aśvattha is the Sanskrit name for Pipal, *Ficus religiosa*, a
relative of the banyan tree. The Sanskrit word *aśvattha* means
"that which will not be tomorrow". This tree outlives most
other trees — it will live on even if the original trunk is
destroyed — but still it does die one day. Here *saṁsāra* is
likened to this tree, for even though it is *avyayam*, long-lived,
it will come to an end when knowledge dawns.

This *saṁsāra* tree must have roots like any other tree.
Generally, we do not see the roots of a tree, but we infer the
existence of the roots because we know that the tree could not
stand without roots holding it in the earth. In the tree of
saṁsāra, the *mūlam*, the taproot, is *ūrdhvam*, upward, meaning
that it is beyond the scope of our immediate perception. That
root is Awareness, which cannot be objectified. It is the
subject because of which we are aware of everything. It is not
something known, but rather the nature of the knower. It is
above the knowledge of one who does not have this teaching.

The branches of this tree are *kṣetra*, the field of experience. The knowledge of *karma* contained in the Vedas forms its leaves, necessary for its survival. Every action is motivated by a desire for a certain result, and a particular action becomes good or bad depending on the subtle, unseen motive that prompted the action. Thus an action, being a physical manifestation of subtle motive, produces not only a gross, visible result, but a subtle, unseen result as well. Both the gross, visible result, *dṛṣṭaphala*, and the subtle, unseen result, *adṛṣṭaphala*, will naturally go to one who entertained the motive and performed the action.

There are two types of *adṛṣṭaphala:* one is a favourable result, *puṇya*, because of which you gain comfort, wealth, position, and so on; the other is *pāpa*, capable of giving you discomforts. *Puṇya* and *pāpa* accrue to the individual who performs actions, and because they must eventually fructify they become the cause of future births. The very knowledge of cause and effect — if I do this, I will get this — is the basis of activity. That activity produces seen and unseen results; the unseen results must be experienced and therefore they produce another birth; in that birth again, activity produces results, and so the cycle of birth and death repeats itself — the tree of *saṁsāra* continues to thrive. Hence, this knowledge of cause and effect, the various means and ends found in the Karmakāṇḍa section of the Vedas, is said to be comparable to the leaves which make the tree live. The one who knows this tree along with its root, who knows the creation and the Awareness that is its basis, knows the meaning of the Vedas.

The Lord continues:

अधश्चोर्ध्वं प्रसृतास्तस्य शाखा
गुणप्रवृद्धा विषयप्रवालाः ।
अधश्च मूलान्यनुसन्ततानि
कर्मानुबन्धीनि मनुष्यलोके ॥ १५-२ ॥

Adhaścordhvaṁ prasṛtāstasya sākhā
.guṇapravṛddhā viṣayapravālāḥ
Adhaśca mūlānyanusantatāni
karmānubandhīni manuṣyaloke (XV:2)

The branches of that tree spread both below and above, strengthened by the *gunas*. The sense objects are its buds.

Its (secondary) roots, born of *karma*, spread downwards in the world of humankind.

Some branches of *saṁsāra* tree go up and some go down, inasmuch as some actions are becoming and some are unbecoming. These actions are influenced by the type of disposition that one enjoys — if one is *sāttvika*, one's values and pursuits will be different from those of a person who is *rājasa* — and so the actions are said to be influenced by *guṇas*. These pursuits are the branches of the tree of *saṁsāra*. Objects in the world are potential branches, the nodular buds out of which new shoots will come, for like dormant buds that suddenly seem to come to life, objects that you never before considered desirable may suddenly crop up as objects of intense desire. Doing these various activities, *jīva* gains good and bad results, including a new body, which performs new actions, gaining new results. These various results are the secondary roots that bind *jīva* to this earth.

Felling the Tree

Even though this tree is described so elaborately, the Lord warns Arjuna against thinking that it has any intrinsic truth. If you analyse it, the whole tree disappears:

न रूपमस्येह तथोपलभ्यते
नान्तो न चादिर्न च सम्प्रतिष्ठा ।
अश्वत्थमेनं सुविरूढमूल–
मसङ्गशस्त्रेण दृढेन छित्त्वा ॥ १५–३ ॥

ततः पदं तत्परिमार्गितव्यं............... ॥ १५–४ ॥

Na rūpamasyeha tathopalabhyate
nānto na cādirna ca sampratīṣṭhā
Aśvatthamenaṁ suvirūḍhamūlaṁ
asaṅgaśastreṇa dṛḍhena chittvā (XV:3)

Tataḥ padaṁ tatparimārgitavyaṁ... (XV:4)

The form of that tree is not perceived here; it has no end, no beginning, and no existence. Having cut this well-rooted *aśvattha* tree with the mighty weapon of detachment, that goal should be sought.

You see a tree; in your mind it is a tree-thought, a thought that has the tree as its object. What is inside that tree-thought? If the name and form of a wave are removed, water alone remains. If you remove the form and name of the tree from the thought, what will remain? Awareness will remain. This is true of any thought: if you remove the pot-name and pot-form from the pot-thought, Awareness alone remains. If you "analyse" any thought, you will find only Awareness. On inquiry all forms and names disappear. The basis of all thoughts is only Awareness.

This is the nature of *saṁsāra* tree and the peculiarity of *māyā*. The tree seems to affect you — it makes you feel limited and sorrowful — but for all that, it is a tree that has no reality. The Lord tells Arjuna that the only way to cast off limitation is to refuse to accept *saṁsāra* as a real tree. Search for the tree, inquire into the nature of the tree, and you will find that the tree recedes from you because you find that there is no tree. This is called *asaṅgaśastra*, the axe of detachment. The detachment required is not physical, for the tree has no reality. The detachment is through knowledge. Know yourself. The wave that knows it is water has no problem of limitation, even though it sees big and small waves all around. Knowledge of yourself as the very root, the very basis of creation, is the goal to be reached.

The End That Never Ends

Lord Kṛṣṇa has described the qualities to be cultivated by the one who seeks knowledge. Similar qualities are mentioned here in the fifteenth chapter:

निर्मानमोहा जितसङ्गदोषा
अध्यात्मनित्या विनिवृत्तकामा: ।
द्वन्द्वैर्विमुक्ता: सुखदु:खसञ्ज्ञै-
र्गच्छन्त्यमूढा: पदमव्ययं तत् ॥ १५-५ ॥

Nirmānamohā jitasaṅgadoṣā
adhyātmanityā vinivṛtta kāmāḥ
Dvandvairvimuktāssukhaduḥkhasañjñair
gacchantyamūḍhāḥ padamavyayaṁ tat (XV:5)

Those who are free from pride and delusion, who have overcome the defect of attachment, who abide in themselves, free from desires, free from the pairs of opposites like misery and happiness — those undeluded people reach that end which is limitlessness.

People, who are no longer deluded by *saṁsāra* because of the knowledge of its structure and its nature, reach the end which never comes to an end. What is that end?

न तद्भासयते सूर्यो न शशाङ्को न पावकः ।
यद्गत्वा न निवर्तन्ते तद्धाम परमं मम ॥ १५–६ ॥

Na tadbhāsayate sūryo na śaśāṅko na pāvakah
Yadgatvā na nivartante taddhāma paramaṁ mama

(XV:6)

There the sun does not shine, nor the moon nor fire. Having reached where no one returns, that is my limitless abode.

Do not take this to mean that the Lord's abode is so dark that no one can find the way out. The Lord's statement means that no source of light is needed to illumine it. Awareness of it is that which illumines all. The sun shines and therefore objects are illumined, but in you the sun, the moon, the stars, and all other sources of light shine. The sun shines because your mind shines; the sun is illumined by your mind. The mind shines because I, Awareness, shines. I shines because I cannot but shine; self — effulgent Awareness shines and everything shines after it. It is *jyotiṣaṁ jyotiḥ* : the light of all lights, the Consciousness because of which everything is known. Therefore, the sun does not shine there; self-effulgent Awareness cannot and need not be illumined by any other source of light. Once you know yourself to be that Awareness, where is the question of return to *saṁsāra*? When knowledge takes place, one cannot remain ignorant, nor can ignorance stage a comeback.

यदादित्यगतं तेजो जगद्भासयतेऽखिलम् ।
यच्चन्द्रमसि यच्चाग्नौ तत्तेजो विद्धि मामकम् ॥ १५--१२ ॥

गामाविश्य च भूतानि धारयाम्यहमोजसा ।
पुष्णामि चौषधीः सर्वाः सोमो भूत्वा रसात्मकः ॥ १५-१३ ॥

Yadādityagataṁ tejo jagadbhāsayate'khilaṁ
Yaccandramasi yaccāgnau tattejo viddhi māmakaṁ
(XV:12)

Gāmāviśya ca bhūtāni dhārayāmyahamojasā
Puṣṇāmi cauṣadhīssarvāssomo bhūtvā rasātmakaḥ (XV:13)

Know that to be my light that resides in the sun and illumines the whole world, that is in the moon and is also in the fire. Having entered the earth, I sustain all beings by my power. Having become the moon, I nourish all the plants.

Lord Kṛṣṇa says, "I am the sun, I am the whole creation; all are in Me. I enter the earth and nourish it, bringing forth the plant and animal kingdoms. I am all the food."

अहं वैश्वानरो भूत्वा प्राणिनां देहमाश्रितः ।
प्राणापानसमायुक्तः पचाम्यन्नं चतुर्विधम् ॥ १५-१४ ॥

Ahaṁ vaiśvānaro bhūtvā prāṇināṁ dehamāśritaḥ
Prāṇāpanasamāyuktaḥ pacāmyannaṁ caturvidhaṁ (XV:14)

Having become the digestive fire, I abide in the bodies of all living beings. Endowed with physiological functions, I digest the fourfold food (*bhakṣyam, bhojyam, coṣyam*, and *lehyam*: that which is chewed, that which is swallowed, that which is sucked, like a mango; and that which is licked, like honey).

The Lord seems to be challenging Arjuna, "I am the sun and the moon and the earth; I am the plants which become your food; the fire in the stomach that digests the food; and also the one who eats the food. Where are you, the so-called *jīva*?"

The Limitless Cannot Be Limited

The nature of *ātmā*, I, is Awareness, limitlessness, which is free from any lack or imperfection. All creation is born of this alone; everything is Awareness. If this is so, why does there seem to be a difference between you and the chair on which you are sitting? If Awareness is all-pervasive, every object should have awareness, should be sentient; but you find that only a few things — plants, animals, human beings etc. — are sentient. There is some rudimentary awareness in plants, there is more evidence of awareness in animals; and human beings seem to enjoy awareness in full measure. Matter, on the other hand, is insentient; a table does not protest against being overburdened; it seems to have no awareness of the load that is piled on it. Why is a stone or a table not aware? How is it that limitless Awareness seems to be confined only to living beings?

Imagine a large clay pot. We can speak of the space inside the pot, because the pot functions as an *upādhi*, a limiting adjunct, for the all-pervasive, unconditioned space; if it is a ten-litre pot, the unconditioned space is conditioned to be a ten-litre space because of this *upādhi*. This is not a real limitation, because the very pot is in space; there is space inside and outside of the walls, and the walls are also in space. Space cannot be limited, but for practical purposes it is. The space in the pot cannot hold more than ten litres of water. In regard to the pot, the space inside it is limited to ten litres; but in truth, in regard to space itself, it is not limited.

Like space, *ātmā*, limitless Awareness, appears to be limited because of *upādhi*. In this case, *upādhi* can consist of gross or subtle matter. To illustrate the meaning of these terms, let us take the case of an incandescent light bulb. In the tungsten filament of the bulb, electricity is converted into light, a form of energy. We know that matter and energy are interchangeable, and hence we can say that the tungsten filament also is energy. To distinguish these two, we can call light subtle energy, and the filament gross energy, or we could call light subtle(*sūkṣma*) matter and the wire gross (*sthūla*) matter.

In comparison to *ātmā* — an existence-Awareness-fullness — everything else, even energy, is *prakṛti*, which is inert; but some *prakṛti* is able to reflect awareness so that it appears sentient. We can call "subtle matter" that *prakṛti* which is able to reflect awareness, and "gross matter" that which cannot. Subtle matter appears conscious and gross matter inert, but the existence enjoyed by each is the same Awareness. Both water and iron can take on the heat of fire, but of the two, only iron can take on the brilliance of the fire too. Similarly, both subtle and gross matter reflect *sat,* the existence that is *ātmā*, but the subtle matter can also reflect *cit,* the Awareness that is *ātmā.*

This physical body, when alive, is capable of experiences; it is sentient. The same body, when dead, is fit only for vultures; it is insentient like any other matter. What really happens at death? You cannot say that *ātmā* has gone away, because that is like saying space has gone away from Bombay to Delhi. *Ananta caitanya,* limitless Awareness, cannot go anywhere. Whatever makes the body sentient must have gone away. Let us call that entity the *sūkṣma-śarīra,* the subtle body, which is matter, but subtle, and capable of reflecting Awareness, as iron is capable of taking on the heat and glow of fire.

In a red hot iron ball, fire and iron are together; one is not laid on the other. Fire is all over the iron ball; every atom of iron is blessed by fire — it is aglow with the heat and brilliance that are the nature of fire. Similarly, your mind, having been blessed by Awareness, is conscious. In turn, the mind makes the sense organs shine, each illumining its corresponding object — forms, tastes, smells, sounds, and touches. When you say, "I am sentient", that I is the subtle body, which is identified with this gross, inert body as fire is identified with the iron ball. The differences between insentient objects and living beings are due to the presence or absence of this subtle body: There is no subtle body in a table; if it were there, the table would be aware and would protest whenever you banged it. *Ātmā,* all-pervasive Awareness, is present in the table, but it is not manifest as consciousness because there is no subtle body in it. In a living being, consciousness is manifest because the subtle body is there; when it leaves, we call the being dead.

The combination of the subtle body and the gross physical body makes a living being. Calcium, carbon, iron, phosphorus, etc. , that make up the gross body, do not make a vivified being. Awareness, reflected in the subtle body, vivifies the physical body. Suppose a man goes to bed and does not wake up in the morning. He does not respond when you try to wake him up. There is no pulse, no breathing: the doctor says he is dead. The subtle body has left the physical body; the tenant has left the tenement. At death, it is not *ātmā* that leaves, but consciousness conditioned by the subtle body leaves the gross body. This conditioned consciousness is known as *jīva*, the one who takes different bodies, according to his or her *karma*.

The Lord continues:

सर्वस्य चाहं हृदि सन्निविष्टो
मत्तः स्मृतिर्ज्ञानमपोहनं च ।
वेदैश्च सर्वैरहमेव वेद्यो
वेदान्तकृद्वेदविदेव चाहम् ॥ १५-१५ ॥

Sarvasya cāhaṁ hṛdi sanniviṣṭo
mattassmṛtirjñānamapohanaṁ ca
Vedaiśca sarvairahameva vedyo
vedāntakṛdvedavideva cāham (XV:15)

I am in all beings, abiding in the heart (in the intellect, as Awareness). Your memory, knowledge, and even your forgetfulness is due to me. I am the one who is to be known through all the scriptures. I am the teacher who teaches Vedanta, and I am (the student who becomes) the one who knows the scriptures.

The Lord here is saying to Arjuna, "I am the first *guru*, the teacher. Since a teacher is a student to begin with, I am the first student also. All knowledge comes from Me, the Lord. I am all things and all knowledge. When as a result of the teaching you know that you are everything, you also are Me."

द्वाविमौ पुरुषौ लोके क्षरश्चाक्षर एव च ।
क्षरः सर्वाणि भूतानि कूटस्थोऽक्षर उच्यते ॥ १५-१६ ॥

उत्तमः पुरुषस्त्वन्यः परमात्मेत्युदाहृतः ।
यो लोकत्रयमाविश्य बिभर्त्यव्यय ईश्वरः ॥ १५-१७ ॥

Dvāvimau puruṣau loke kṣaraścākṣara eva ca
Kṣarassarvāṇi bhūtāni kūṭastho'kṣara ucyate (XV:16)

Uttamaḥ puruṣastvanyaḥ paramātmetyudahṛtaḥ
Yo lokatrayamāviśya bibhartyavyaya īśvaraḥ (XV:17)

In this world there are two types of *puruṣas* or Self: *kṣara*, the changing; and *akṣara*, the changeless. All beings subject to change are called *kṣara*, and that which is changeless is called *akṣara*. The most exalted *puruṣa* is another (other than these two). He is called *paramātmā*. Having entered the three worlds, that unchanging Lord sustains all.

The Lord explains, "This entire creation, including your physical body, is *kṣara,* subject to change. The cause from which the changing world is born is called *akṣara*, the changeless. It is only with reference to the changing that I am called the changeless being. In reality, with reference only to Myself, I am beyond both *kṣara* and *akṣara*. I am *puruṣottama*; I am *brahman* that abides in all, pervading and sustaining all the three worlds, gross, subtle, and causal. "

19

The Divine and the Demoniac Nature

Programming, Values, and Virtues

A human being has a mind potentially capable of knowing, analysing, and assimilating experiences. He or she is endowed with the ability to think and to know independently, unlike animals, who are totally programmed and subject to further programming. A chimpanzee can be trained to drive a motorcycle, but it will not get down and ask for a Coke, or count the change. The capacity to think, to analyse, to conclude is unique to mankind. A person may be programmed by *karma* to be born in a given place, to have a certain type of *upādhi*, to meet with certain situations; but his or her thinking is definitely not programmed. If it were, learning, as we find in human beings, would not be possible.

A man can, however, subject himself to programming; he can condition himself to think that he alone is right; he may become an idealist who will even destroy society for the sake of his ideal. A fanatic is like this; he has sacrificed his reason at the altar of some cause. But a person can also keep reason under control. The Lord says that if one's faculty of reasoning is kept always in a fluid state, ready to give up the old and absorb new ideas, one will become divine.

As a child one is subject to being programmed by parents, teachers, or society, because one has not yet developed reasoning. You learn that you should respect the learned and the elders; that you should not steal or lie. You do not fully appreciate these values when they are told you in your childhood, but you follow the rules because you are so told. You oblige your father, mother, religion, and state, and honour the basic values of speaking the truth, following the path of righteousness, respecting parents and teachers, not doing bad deeds, not drinking alcohol or eating meat, not hurting any being.

Once grown up, however, you can think independently and you assimilate the values that will guide you in deciding what is right and wrong; because if you do not assimilate these values properly, if they do not become your values, following them would be by way of obliging others all the time. No one can do that and so when it is inconvenient to follow the rules you were taught, you will give them up. Everytime you do any of these things out of obligation to others, without having assimilated the value behind your action, the hour of compromise moves closer. If values remain as the result of programming rather than having become assimilated virtues, an occasion will come when you will cast these values aside

Suppose you have been hungry for three days. Would you pick food out of garbage and eat it? You would not; but it is not because you are obliging the health department by adopting their principles of hygiene. It is because you have a very well assimilated value for eating only clean, fresh food. Similarly, one must come to speak the truth, not hurt others, and so on, not as a result of any conditioning but because such behaviour is one's nature.

In the sixteenth chapter we find a list of virtues to be cultivated by a seeker of knowledge. The Lord tells Arjuna that a person who has truly assimilated these values has *daivi sampat*, a divine nature.

अभयं सत्त्वसंशुद्धिर्ज्ञानयोगव्यवस्थितिः ।
दानं दमश्च यज्ञश्च स्वाध्यायस्तप आर्जवम् ॥ १६–१ ॥

अहिंसा सत्यमक्रोधस्त्यागः शान्तिरपैशुनम् ।
दया भूतेष्वलोलुप्त्वं मार्दवं ह्रीरचापलम् ॥ १६–२ ॥

तेजः क्षमा धृतिः शौचमद्रोहो नातिमानिता ।
भवन्ति सम्पदं दैवीमभिजातस्य भारत ॥ १६–३ ॥

Abhayaṁ sattvasaṁśuddhirjñānayogavyāvasthitiḥ
Dānaṁ ḍamaśca yajñāśca svādhyāystapa ārjavaṁ (XVI:1)

Ahiṁsā satyamakrodhastyāgaśśāntirapaiśunaṁ
Dayā bhūteṣvaloluptvaṁ mārdavaṁ hrīracāpalaṁ (XVI:2)

Tejaḥ Kṣamā dhṛtiśśaucamadroho nātimānitā
Bhavanti sampadaṁ daivīmabhijātasya bhārata (XVI:3)

Fearlessness, purity of mind, commitment to (the pursuit of) knowledge and *yoga*, charitableness, self-restraint, doing worship, study of the scriptures, performing austerities, straightforwardness, practice of noninjury, truthfulness, controlling anger, renunciation, tranquillity, not speaking ill of others, compassion for all beings, lack of desire for objects, gentleness, modesty, not speaking or acting needlessly, brilliance of mind, not reacting internally to attack or accusation, fortitude, purity of body and mind, absence of desire to harm anyone, absence of pride — these qualities belong to one whose nature is divine.

Assimilating Values

To assimilate a value is to see its intrinsic nature — speaking the truth, for example, not because somebody has told you to but because you see the value of doing so. If you tell a lie, you create a split within yourself. When you speak, you are an actor; when you think, you are a thinker. If what you say is different from what you think, you are slowly creating a gulf between the thinker and the actor; and a time will come when you will think of doing something and there will be no one to carry out the action. That is why even though you decide at night to get up early the next morning, you are not able to do it. The mind registers your wish, waking you even before the alarm bell rings, but when it does ring, you bang it down and go back to sleep. Why? The thinker is different from the actor; you become a Dr. Jekyll and Mr. Hyde. You have good intentions, but these are not enough if there is a gap between the thinker and the doer. You will find that you cannot accomplish even simple things here on earth; how can you then hope to reach the Lord ever?

Let us consider another value, *ahiṁsā*, noninjury. What does it mean to assimilate this value? You want to live and live happily; your neighbour also wants to do the same. He does not want you to hurt him, and you do not want him to hurt you. Sage Vyāsa has written in the Mahābhārata that you should not do unto others what you do not want them to do to you, whatever treatment you want from others, that you should give them. This is the commonsense basis of all *dharma*; if you assimilate this one value fully, all other values will follow, just as if you pull one leg of a bed, the other three will follow. Practising this "golden rule", one becomes sensitive to the needs of others as towards those of one's own.

One need not be a saint to have these virtues; anyone can cultivate them. If you follow these values, not to oblige someone else but to oblige yourself, you become divine, that is, you become a complete human being. Those who do not assimilate these values will have instead *āsura-bhāva*, demoniac qualities. Lord Kṛṣṇa tells Arjuna:

दम्भो दर्पोऽभिमानश्च क्रोधः पारुष्यमेव च ।
अज्ञानं चाभिजातस्य पार्थ सम्पदमासुरीम् ॥ १६–४ ॥

Dambho darpo'bhimānaśca krodhaḥ pāruṣyameva ca
Ajñānaṁ cābhijātasya pārtha sampadamāsurīṁ (XVI:4)

Pretentiousness, vanity, self-conceit, anger, harshness, and ignorance of right and wrong — these qualities belong to one whose nature is demoniac.

Lord Kṛṣṇa continues with his description of *āsura-bhāva:*

आढ्योऽभिजनवानस्मि कोऽन्योऽस्ति सदृशो मया ।
यक्ष्ये दास्यामि मोदिष्य इत्यज्ञानविमोहिताः ॥ १६–१५ ॥

Adhyo'bhijanavānasmi ko'nyo'sti sadṛśo mayā
Yakṣye dāsyāmi modiṣya ityajñānavimohitāḥ (XVI:15)

"I am rich, I am well-born; who else is equal to me? I will perform all sacrifices, I will give to others, I will rejoice" — so say those thoroughly deluded by ignorance.

One who has this sort of bloated *ahankara*, ego, is *asura*, a demon. The taller your claims, the greater your ignorance, because you depend upon so many for what you are and what you accomplish in this world. If one does not appreciate this, one is *asura*.

Asura is not necessarily one with prominent canine teeth. Behind a pleasing form one can be all vulgarity, motivated by false values. To be truly human one must assimilate moral nd ethical values as one matures. This involves questioning the values that have been taught by one's religion, one's father and mother, one's teachers. Having examined a value to determine its worth, one may use it or give it up; but too often you throw away values without understanding them, or they are lost because you have not assimilated them — they only float in your mind when you are a child, to be thrown away as you grow older. Examine each value and assimilate it so that by following it you are obliging not God or anyone else, but only yourself. This will make you truly human, a person who is easy to relate to. No one can relate to a person who is like a tiger, a cat, a donkey, a scorpion, a cobra all in one; because even that person does not know what he or she will be like at a particular time. A pouncing tiger is not bad, because pouncing is its nature; but if a man pounces, it is a problem. If he is unable to check his animal instincts, it is because he has not assimilated the ethical and moral values that make him a human being.

Values for Liberation

Only a person who has assimilated these values will have the mental poise and dispassion required for the study of Vedanta. Therefore, Lord Kṛṣṇa says that these values will lead one to liberation:

दैवी सम्पद्विमोक्षाय निबन्धायासुरी मता ।
मा शुचः सम्पदं दैवीमभिजातोऽसि पाण्डव ॥ १६–५ ॥

Daivī sampadvimokṣāya nibandhāyāsuri matā
Mā śucassampadaṁ daivīmabhijāto'si pāṇḍava (XVI:5)

The divine attributes are considered the means of liberation, the demoniac of bondage. Do not fear, Arjuna; you are born to a divine nature.

Lord Kṛṣṇa's meaning is: "These divine attributes which make you human are the means of discovering freedom. If a person has these values, he or she will become naturally calm, with an abiding mind free from likes and dislikes. That mind can own up the teaching that one is all fullness, freedom, joy — all that one is fundamentally interested in achieving. Understand, Arjuna, that you have these qualities."

20
The Threefold Śraddhā

The seventeenth chapter begins with another question from Arjuna. Lord Kṛṣṇa has explained the three types of human disposition — *sāttvika, rājasa,* and *tāmasa* — and the two types of value systems — divine and demoniac. Arjuna wonders how to categorise the people who have *śraddhā,* faith, in the scriptures, but for some reason do not perform worship as stipulated in the scriptures. He asks the Lord, "How does one categorise those who worship, but not according to the method stipulated in the scriptures?"

In reply, the Lord says that faith is of three types. From the type of prayers that one offers or the altar one chooses to worship, you can decide whether someone's *śraddhā is sāttvikī, rājasī,* or *tāmasī.* One who worships spirits and goes to the cremation ground to perform penance to destroy others, has only *tāmasī-śraddhā.* One who wants to become powerful and worships to become greater than another fellow has *rājasī-śraddhā.* He may perform severe penance for obtaining even small things in life. Nobody performed *tapas* more determinedly than Rāvaṇa did, but he still remained only a demon — the *tapas* did not change him. Lastly, one who wants to purify his or her mind and worships for this purpose has *sāttvikī-śraddhā.* This type of *śraddhā* is in keeping with the scriptures. Any Hindu ritual or worship begins with a *saṅkalpa*, a statement of purpose. One says, "I have committed sins, knowingly and unknowingly. For eliminating them, for purifying my mind, and for gaining the grace of the Lord, I am performing this ritual. Though the Lord abides in my heart, I do not see Him; by this action may I come to see Him." The attitude represented by these words is *sāttvikī-śraddhā.*

The Lord goes on to explain that the religious actions of performing penance and giving charity can also be categorised according to guṇas:

यज्ञस्तपस्तथा दानं तेषां भेदमिमं शृणु ॥ १७–७ ॥

Yajñastapastathā dānaṁ teṣāṁ bhedamimaṁ śṛṇu

(XVII:7)

Listen while I describe to you the different types of ritual, penance and charity.

Tapas, the performance of austerities, may be an activity of the mind, the speech, or the body. If one deliberately tries to maintain a mind that is silent or cheerful or aler , the effort is called *mānasa-tapas,* mental austerity. If one is deliberate in speaking, making sure one's words are true, gentle and meaningful, one is practising *vāk-tapas,* austerity of speech. Exerting control over one's sense.organs and body is called *kāyika-tapas*, physical austerity. As in the case of *śraddhā*, any of these types of *tapas* can be *sāttvika, rājasa,* or *tāmasa,* according to the motive one has in doing it.

Dānam, giving charity, can also be of three types. *Sāttvika-dānam* is a gift freely given by one who is able to give, to one who is deserving of the gift. One who is able to give is rich; not necessarily one who has money. However much one may have, one is poor if one cannot part with it; and a person who has only one rupee is rich if he or she is ready to give it to a needy person. If you cannot use your riches, if you cannot spend them where they are needed, you are not rich. Therefore, the Lord says, "May you give whatever is to be given. Don't think about it — give, wash your hands of the gift, and forget that you gave it." A gift is truly a gift if it blesses the one who receives it, rather than make him or her feel obliged to the giver. When you give you must also see that the one to whom you give deserves the gift. Do not give it to a drunkard who will only drink it away; such a gift will not be a blessing to anyone.

Giving with a cameraman around, publicising your charity for furthering your own ends, is *rājasa-dānam. Tāmasa-dānam* is charity done to destroy others, or that given without knowledge of its purpose or its recipient.

Lord Kṛṣṇa assures Arjuna, "The values that I have taught you are *sāttvika* values. When assimilated they will make you naturally contemplative, and you will therefore know Me as yourself. I abide in all; in Me everything exists; you and I are not different at all. This truth becomes clear to one whose mind is mature, simple, cool, rich, accommodative, and ready to accept limitations; a mind that has nothing to long for or hate, that is abiding. Such a mind is not distinct from me; I am that mind. With that mind you will see the truth of what I have taught. You will discover that you are *sat-cit-ānanda.*

21
The Result of the Teaching

The final chapter of the Gita begins with Arjuna asking Lord Kṛṣṇa to explain to him *sannyāsa* and *tyāga.* Both the words mean renunciation and they have been the subject matter of the entire Gita. Arjuna no longer asks which is superior, *karma yoga* or *sannyāsa*; instead he wants to know what difference there is —if any — between *sannyāsa* and *tyāga,* two words that the Lord has been using throughout his teaching, sometimes interchangeably, sometimes differently. In answering him, the Lord sums up the teaching that we have been following in all the previous chapters.

Tyāga : Renunciation of the Fruit of Action

The Lord says that *tyāga* is *karma-phala-tyāga,* giving up the fruit of actions, also called *karma yoga.* As a *karma-yogī,* you perform an action because it is your responsibility. You do expect the result — nobody performs action without expecting some outcome — but it does not affect you whether the result is what you expected or not, because you receive any result as *prasāda,* a blessing from the Lord. You recognise that you have not created the laws by which the result is determined; the Lord shapes the laws, and so you see the result as coming from Him and receive it with glad acceptance. Even a *kāmya-karma,* a desire-prompted action, can be *yoga* if you have this attitude toward its result. This is *karma-phala-tyāga,* renouncing the fruits of action.

Sannyāsa : Renunciation of Action

There are three types of *sannyāsa* — *āpat-sannyāsa, vividiṣā-sannyāsa,* and *vidvat- sannyāsa.* The *āpat-sannyāsī* renounces everything when he is about to die; he gives up when the doctors have given up. For a Hindu, life is divided into four *āśramas*, or stages of life: *brahmacarya*, the life of a student; *gṛhasthya*, the life of a householder; *vānaprastha*, the life of a forest dweller; and *sannyāsa*, the life of renunciation. A man who is about to die has a choice to take *sannyāsa* so that whatever benefit that is associated with this fourth stage can come to him. He is taken from his house and placed in a cottage; when he dies, as a *sannyāsī* he will be buried, instead of being cremated with the usual rites. This is called *āpat-sannyāsa*, a *sannyāsa* at the time of danger — and it is a dangerous *sannyāsa*. Should the man recover from his illness, he will not know what to do with his new status. He still has a lot of worldly concerns; he is full of likes and dislikes; he does not want to leave his house or wife. Thus the order of *sannyāsa* itself is in danger because it has been taken by a person whose mind is not ready for it.

The second type of *sannyāsa* is called *vividiṣā-sannyāsa*. This is the *sannyāsa* that has been contrasted to *karma yoga* all through the Gita. *Vividiṣā* means "desire to know". A person who is not interested in pleasure in this world or in heaven may take *sannyāsa* in order to pursue knowledge. This type of *sannyāsa* is also dangerous, because, like *āpat-sannyāsa*, it is taken for the wrong reason, and therefore may not be natural. A person who still holds a value for objects, wealth, or security is not ready for *sannyāsa*.

The Taste Remains

The value we attach to objects is two-fold: an intellectual value, and a habitual value. An intellectual value may be subjective or objective. Gold has a well-defined objective value, but if you have a special attachment for a gold wedding ring, for you the ring holds a much greater value than what it would be in the marketplace. You attribute an extra value of sanctity to it, but this extra value does not belong to the gold — it is a subjective value, the creation of your mind. If you use that same mind to inquire into the ring and appreciate it for what it is, its subjective value disappears and only the objective value remains — you see the object as it really is. This is what happens when you study the Gita. You see the world as it really is, not as it is coloured by your likes and dislikes.

Even after you have come to see a thing objectively, you may find that you continue to pursue that thing; this is due to its habitual value. Even when an alcoholic comes to know that drinking is dangerous, he is not able to remain without alcohol, because he has a habitual value for it. Because of habit, he is helpless. That is what the Lord means when he says that the taste for objects remains — as either an intellectual or a habitual value — even though a person might abstain from any contact with the objects.

Lord Kṛṣṇa tells Arjuna that mere renunciation of action does not qualify an unprepared person to become a *sannyāsī*. One cannot become a *sannyāsī* so long as one has a large stock of likes and dislikes. To rid onself of likes and dislikes one must pursue *karma yoga*, and one cannot perform action while one is a *sannyāsī*. A *sannyāsī* can perform only those actions enjoined on him; he cannot start a business or get married. So, if he takes *sannyāsa* without qualifying for it, he becomes *ubhayabhraṣṭa*, fallen from both *yoga* and *sannyāsa*, he is neither here nor there. Therefore, Lord Kṛṣṇa advises Arjuna, "Be a *karma-yogī* even though you are longing to renounce all your obligations and leave this war."

The World Is Not a Trap

If you are uneasy in a situation and want to get out of it, it is better that you continue in that same field and master it. Taking *sannyāsa* is getting away from the field by your own volition; you hope that you will be able to meditate, once you are rid of this world. If you want to quit because you think the world is too much with you, stay in the world, prove yourself, see that the world cannot hurt you any more. If you feel that the world is a trap, you should examine yourself, because the same world does not seem to make everybody else unhappy. Perhaps your unhappiness is your own creation — you have made the world a monster; it is only a projection of your mind. The world does not produce sorrow; it only produces experiences for you. If you derive sorrow from these, the problem lies with you and not with the world. When you point a finger of accusation at the world, the other fingers point at you. As a bad tooth converts food to poison, your mind makes your life a sad affair.

Sadness Is Worked Up

Reasons for sadness vary but sadness is the same for everyone. An old Tamil verse tells of four people talking of their sorrows: One says, "I am so poor that I cannot have salt for my gruel, so I am sorrowful;" another says, "I have milk, but I don't have sugar for it, therefore I am sorrowful;" the third says, "I don't have a pair of shoes, so I am sorrowful"; and the fourth adds, "I am sorrowful because my palanquin does not have any cushions in it. "

There is no salt or sugar or shoes or cushions in sadness. The sadness of all these people is the same, even though the means of removing it differ. A beggar who has lost his begging bowl will be happy if he gets a begging bowl, but a king who has lost his kingdom is not going to be cheered up by getting a begging bowl.

The Lord teaches Arjuna that sorrow is a result of mental projection. He says, "*Aśocyān anvaśocastvam*: You are grieving for that which deserves no grief. You have a lot of information, but you do not have much wisdom about life. You are a master of warfare, logistics, archery, dance, and music, but you do not have the knowledge that converts a sorrowful life into a happy one. Please understand, Arjuna, there is no legitimate cause for your sorrow. "

Sorrow does not happen; you contrive it. When you hear the news of someone's death, you are only shocked; only after the news sinks in does sorrow slowly develop. Like jealousy and other emotions, sorrow is built up. Happiness is natural to you, sorrow is not. If sorrow were natural, you would be happily sorrowful; but you want to get rid of it, and you can get rid of it, because it does not belong to you. Though it looks as if happiness comes and goes, it does not. It is only that your confused thoughts sometimes keep you from enjoying the happiness that you are. You think that this world makes you sorrowful, and that giving it up will help you; but you cannot give up the world totally as long as you are alive. What the Lord has said earlier — "*Na hi kaścit kṣaṇamapi jātu tiṣṭhatyakarmakṛt:* No one can remain without activity even for a moment" — he repeats now in other words:

न हि देहभृता शक्यं त्यक्तुं कर्माण्यशेषतः ।
यस्तु कर्मफलत्यागी स त्यागीत्यभिधीयते ॥ १८–११ ॥

Nahi dehabhṛtā śakyaṁ tyaktuṁ karmāṇyaśeṣataḥ
Yastu karmaphalatyāgī sa tyāgītyabhidhīyate (XVIII:11)

Indeed, one who dwells in the body cannot give up actions completely. The one who gives up the results of actions is known as a renouncer.

It is possible for one to give up some particular actions, but not all actions, as long as one is alive. Therefore, *tyāga* means *karma phala tyāga.* Perform actions but renounce the results; take them as they come. In the process your likes and dislikes will be neutralised, and in time your mind will become pure.

The Lord's Offer

A teacher can tell from his or her eyes, if a student has understood and the Lord knows that his words to Arjuna have reached home. With the confidence of a good teacher who knows his student, he gives Arjuna freedom of choice, telling him to do whatever he thinks proper:

इति ते ज्ञानमाख्यातं गुह्याद्गुह्यतरं मया ।
विमृश्यैतदशेषेण यथेच्छसि तथा कुरु ॥ १८–६३ ॥

Iti te jñānamākhyātaṁ guhyādguhyataraṁ mayā
Vimṛśyaitadaśeṣeṇa yathecchasi tathā kuru (XVIII:63)

This knowledge that is most secret has been told you by Me. Having inquired into it thoroughly, may you do as you wish.

The Lord offers Arjuna a choice: "If you want to give up action, fine; if you want to lead a life of *karma yoga,* that is also fine." Lord Kṛṣṇa says this because he knows very well that Arjuna has understood.

Summing up the Teaching

Before concluding the discourse, the Lord sums up the teaching:

सर्वगुह्यतमं भूयः शृणु मे परमं वचः ।
इष्टोऽसि मे दृढमिति ततो वक्ष्यामि ते हितम् ॥ १८–६४ ॥

Sarvaguhyatamaṁ bhūyaśśṛnu me paramam vacaḥ
Iṣṭo'sime dṛḍhamiti tato vakṣyāmi te hitaṁ (XVIII:64)

Please listen again to My exalted words that are the greatest secret of all. You are very dear to Me, without doubt; therefore I will tell you what is good for you.

Lord Kṛṣṇa lovingly speaks to Arjuna,"Now I will give you the essence of all I have said, because I have great love for you, for you are not only my friend, but also my disciple.

"I have already unfolded *rāja-guhyam*, the king among secrets, for your appreciation, but now I am going to focus on it again. I know that you have understood Me, but I will sum up everything now to be sure that you have not missed the vision in a maze of words. "

Like a vulture which, though flying high, keeps its eyes glued on its prey on the ground far below, the teacher has his eyes fixed on the subject of teaching. Though he may touch on many topics and use many illustrations, he will point out the truth again and again.

Summing up the teaching, the Lord says,

मन्मना भव मद्भक्तो मद्याजी मां नमस्कुरु ।
मामेवैष्यसि सत्यं ते प्रतिजाने प्रियोऽसि मे ॥ १८–६५ ॥

Manmanā bhava madbhakto madyājī māṁ namaskuru
Māmevaiṣyasi satyaṁ te pratijāne priyo'si me
(XVIII:65)

May you become one whose mind is ever in Me, who is devoted to Me, who worships Me; may you prostrate yourself before Me. You shall reach Me alone. I promise you this is true, for you are dear to Me.

You come into this world as a guest entering a guest house. You do not bring a truckload of supplies, but bring only the carry-on baggage of the physical body. You know that you will be well taken care of. Look up at the sky; what a beautiful ceiling, with everchanging colours. Your eyes see a riot of colours; your ears hear symphonies and the song of birds, you smell the scents of jasmine and rose; and there are things beyond your sense organs which you can discover and enjoy with your intellect. Everything is provided for your comfort and enjoyment; you need only to make use of it. If in such a guest house one thinks one is sad, it must be a mistake.

When your stay here in this guest house is over, you leave it as it was when you arrived. You do not possess anything here, nor do you take anything with you when you go. This guest house of the world is meant for you as long as you are here, and then you leave it to others. You make your stay a pleasant one and leave with pleasant memories.

In all this you cannot miss the hand of the benevolent host who has provided for your stay. In the beautiful flowers and lakes, in the entire creation, you see only Him. Your thanks go to Him who made all this; your salutations go to Him alone.

Thus the Lord advises Arjuna, "Appreciate Me in all your perceptions; thereby may you be My devotee. Do not be an occasional devotee suffering from bouts of devotion. Do not fall at the feet of one or the other altar. Devotion to Me is not a matter of feeling, but a matter of discovery, as a scientist discovers a fact. Let Me be the altar where you dedicate all your action. This attitude is *karma yoga*, and this will make you a *sannyāsī*, one who knows oneself to be one with Me."

सर्वधर्मान्परित्यज्य मामेकं शरणं व्रज ।
अहं त्वा सर्वपापेभ्यो मोक्षयिष्यामि मा शुचः ॥ १८–६६ ॥

Sarvadharmān parityajya māmekaṁ śaraṇaṁ vraja
Ahaṁ tvā sarvapāpebhyo mokṣayiṣyāmi mā śucaḥ

(XVIII:66)

Giving up all actions, seek Me as your sole refuge. I will liberate you from all sins; do not grieve.

This is the last verse of the teaching of Lord Kṛṣṇa. Here the word *dharma* means *karma*, action, because action includes both *dharma* and *adharma*, good and bad. "Giving up all actions come to Me."

Arjuna might have asked,"But how is that possible? You have told me several times that no one can give up *all* activities." The Lord's meaning is: "You need not literally give up action, because you never perform any action. Understand that even while performing action you are actionless — this knowledge is the only way to give up all actions. "

All actions take place in the presence of the I. The sense organs and the body perform actions — seeing, going, coming, taking, talking — but the I is always actionless. This knowledge is real *sannyāsa*, called *naiṣkarmya-siddhi*, the achievement of actionlessness. A *vidvān*, a person who has this knowledge and who follows the life of renunciation, is living the third type of *sannyāsa*, *vidvatsannyāsa*, renunciation characterised by knowledge.

Thus the Lord completes his teaching by reminding Arjuna of all He has said,"You have been performing action with the attitude that you are the *kartā*, doer; now do what must be done with the attitude of *karma yoga*, seeing that I am the *kṣetrajña* abiding in you. I abide in all beings, and in Me all beings abide. I am *sat-cit-ānanda*. I am Awareness in you. Appreciate Me in this manner, and I shall liberate you from all sins; you will discover yourself to be actionless. "

Lord Kṛṣṇa had introduced the teaching at the beginning, "*Aśocyān anvaśocastvam*: You grieve over things that deserve no grief." Now he concludes the teaching with this statement: "*Mā śucah*: Have no grief." The unity between the introduction and conclusion shows the master teacher that Lord Kṛṣṇa is. He told Arjuna at the beginning that he was grieving for no reason. He has now proved the truth of his statement, "Do not grieve."

Arjuna's Response

In response to the teaching, Arjuna says:

नष्टो मोहः स्मृतिर्लब्धा त्वत्प्रसादान्मयाच्युत ।
स्थितोऽस्मि गतसन्देहः करिष्ये वचनं तव ॥ १८–७३ ॥

Naṣṭo mohassmṛtirlabdhā tvatprasādānmayācyuta
Sthito'smi *gatasandehaḥ kariṣye vacanaṁ tava*

(XVIII:73)

My delusion is destroyed; knowledge has been gained by

me through Your grace, O Acyuta. I am firm, my doubts are gone. I will do as you say.

Arjuna's answer reveals his understanding, "Once I was confused about what is right and what is wrong. Now those confused thoughts that floated in my mind are gone. I have come back to myself; I have a vision of myself. I know that I am full. Before this teaching I experienced fullness only in moments of happiness, never knowing that I was looking at myself at those moments. Now I know that I am happiness, free from longings, cravings, likes and dislikes, and the desire to be different. What was once a momentary experience is now abiding knowledge. You have made me see this very clearly. My ignorance is gone. Because of Your grace I have gained all this, O Lord!

"I am now firm on my feet; I stand where I should. You have removed all my doubts. I will do what you have told me — I will take up my bow and fight. I know I am neither the slayer, nor the slain. I am happily seated in this body, never performing action. Dhṛtarāṣṭra will see what is going to happen. Let *dharma* be established. "

Conclusion

With Arjuna's words, the dialogue between teacher and student is over. Now the Bhagavad Gita is concluded with these words of Sanjaya to Dhṛtarāṣṭra:

यत्र योगेश्वरः कृष्णो यत्र पार्थो धनुर्धरः ।
तत्र श्रीर्विजयो भूतिर्ध्रुवा नीतिर्मतिर्मम ॥ १८-७८ ॥

Yatra yogeśvaraḥ kṛṣṇo yatra pārtho dhanurdharaḥ
Tatra śrīrvijayo bhūtirdhruvā nītirmatirmama

(XVIII:78)

Where Kṛṣṇa, the Lord of all *yogīs'*, is, where Arjuna is wielding his bow, there will be bountiful wealth, victory, prosperity and justice that never wavers. This is my conviction.

Sañjaya feels that he is most fortunate to have heard Lord Kṛṣṇa's teaching. He tells Dhṛtarāṣṭra,"I shudder with delight and rejoice again and again, recalling this wondrous discourse. "

The dialogue of Lord Kṛṣṇa and Arjuna will shine through all posterity; it will never become obsolete for its relevance is universal and timeless. Where Śri Kṛṣṇa and Arjuna are, or where knowledge joins with right attitude and action, there wealth, victory and glory shall be. This is the teaching of the Bhagavad Gita.

Om Tat Sat